Beginners Guide to Fasting Lifestyle

Lose Weight and Manage Diabete

Authors
Treena J. Cox

Table of Contents Section One: Introduction Chapter 1

C   1

Fasting has been tested over time as an ancient tradition; it improves concentration, prolongs life, prevents Alzheimer, and insulin resistance; equally reverses the aging process.

In case you don't know yet, about the broad nature of fasting, you'd be shocked to learn and discover lots of things that may propel you to want to consider fasting sooner.

It is not yet clear who introduced fasting, but men began fasting thousands of years ago. Fasting is prominent among the oldest healing medications. And as a universal human instinct, it is as old as humankind itself.

Historically, ancient doctors recommended fasting as a significant part of ailment prevention and cures.

Hippocrates, the man referred to as the father of Western medicine believed that fasting helps the body rebuild itself naturally.

Paracelsus, another renowned authority in ancient Western traditional medicine, over 500 years ago noted that "fasting is the greatest remedy, the physician within."

Let me also remind you that **Ayurvedic** medicine is among the oldest advocate of fasting as a necessary treatment.

Pythagoras of ancient Greece also promoted the importance of fasting. And around the 14th century, St Catherine of Siena practically popularized fasting, just as revival doctor, Paracelsus, refers to it as "physician within."

WHAT IS FASTING?

What then is **fasting**? For this book, fasting is the voluntary abstinence of food (with or without fluid intake) for personal reasons, including religious, political, social, and health motives.

Irrespective of your motive for fasting, there's a consensus on the distinguished benefit of fasting across-board, as devotees of one religion or the other have all professed that it gives one physical and spiritual renaissance.

Fasting for divine purposes

Widely experienced by devotees of the different religious sects, fasting for divine purposes will continue to be an integral part of all major religions globally. Religious figures like Jesus Christ, Prophet Muhammad, and Buddha all agreed on the efficacy and the healing authority of fasting.

Usually referred to as a cleansing or purification period, fasting is mainstream to practically all religious practices.

It is believed that fasting independently grew across cultures and religions, either because of its health importance to the body or for spiritual benefit.

Examining how the different religious groups approach fasting, an independent study indicated that Buddhism requires followers to take food in the morning till the next morning, every day. Sometimes drinking of water-alone for days and perhaps weeks are adopted as a method of fasting.

Christians may follow a different fasting pattern because of their sectarian nature, but the Greek orthodox Christians have a fasting plan that spans up to 200 days in a year. It's a spiritual discipline, according to the Bible.

Muslims will fast from sunrise to sunset in their holy month known as the Ramadan fasting; in addition to the Monday and Thursdays fast promoted by prophet Mohamed, expected to hold every week.

Experts took a particular interest in Ramadan fasting because its peculiar fasting protocol forbids fluid intake within the stipulated fasting period.

With a short period of mild dehydration, eating is only allowed before sunrise and past sunset. A study recently suggested that daily caloric consumption increases within this period because usually, adherent overeats before and after the fast.

Therefore, fasting has stood through the ages and has significantly maintained its importance till today. Still, the best way to appreciate the physiology of fasting is to understand its **therapeutic dietary** help in fighting disease in the human body.

An overview of fasting

Fasting for healthy living or religious reasons will provide similar results like **weight loss:** with an average of 0.9kg leaving the body within the first week of commencement and reduced to about 0.3kg by the third week.

This high reduction of weight is mainly because of negative sodium balance. There is a metabolically high rate of **gluconeogenesis**: amino acids being the significant substrates.

And with enlistment and oxidation occurring as you progress on the fasting and progressive ketosis developing, the ketone increases to take the place of glucose as the primary energy source of the central nervous system; and subsequently diminishing the need for gluconeogenesis and a scanty protein breakdown.

It's an established truth that many **hormonal changes** occur while fasting; there is also a reduction in Insulin level. Is this the reason why most studies in fasting have always used obese people? I have to say that the outcome may not apply to lean people because it requires further research.

Medical experts have also identified gout and urate nephrolithiasis, cardiac arrhythmias, and postural hypotension as inherent side effects or complications resulting from fasting.

How Fasting Started: A Brief History

Some ancient culture records indicate that fasting was used as a pre-war preparation ritual, while others used it as a means of coming-of-age practices.

And still, others will declare fasting to appease an angry god; notably, the native north Americans used fasting to escape collective calamities like famine.

Apart from Zoroastrianism that does not allow fasting, all the world religions incorporate fasting as a critical idea in achieving different kinds of self-control and as an act of contrition.

For instance, Judaism has many yearly fasting days like the **Yom Kippur** and the Day of Atonement. **Islam** also has its annual fasting days: the Holy month of Ramadan. In Christianity, the Roman Catholic, the Eastern orthodoxy observe 40 days fasting period known as Lent.

"Anorexia mirabilis" is a term used to describe women's appetite for spiritual fasting (amazingly losing the desire for food).

Many religions generally see fasting as a mark of consecration and chastity; commenting on the spiritual benefits of fasting, an English anchoress and spiritualist in the 14th century noted that fasting is a way of communicating with Jesus Christ.

Specific belief systems will tell you that the gods will show you divine dreams and visions after successful fasting. Fasting also has a history of being used as a tool for advancing a political cause.

Mahatma Gandhi's activities come to mind here: in his struggle to liberate Indians from the British-imposed tax was reported to have embarked on fasting for a period of 21days.

Worthy of note with Mahatma Gandhi's fasting is that he ate vegetarian food while embarking on prolonged fasting for self-purification and social protest.

The possible downside of fasting is fraudsters use it negatively to exploit the gullible in society. The activities of one "Doctor" **Linda Burfield Hazard** *of Minnesota* that led to the death of more than 40 patients, erroneously made to engage in fasting in 1912, readily comes to mind. History recorded that she also died of fasting in 1938.

Recall also the Victorian "fasting girls" who bragged their ability to do without food, especially Sarah Jacobs, who was at age 12 confirmed to have died of starvation.

Therapeutic fasting

When you go into a fasting mood, with the sole aim of treating or preventing ill health, following medical advice; it's known as Therapeutic fasting.

This fasting pattern was popularized in the United States sometime in the 19th century by **Dr. Herbert Shelton** with the "natural Hygiene Movement."

Talking about how he was able to make about 40,000 patients regain their health with only-water fasting, Dr. Shelton notes thus,

---

"Fasting must be recognized as a fundamental and radical process that is older than any other mode of caring for the sick organism, for it is employed on the plane of instinct."

Apart from being a strong advocate of **alternative medicine,** recall that Shelton was appointed by the American Vegetarian Party as its presidential candidate in 1956 for the United States election.

Though he is an advocate of **original natural hygiene,** critics have described such an idea as mere quackery.

"Nature cure," as it's often called in the UK, incorporated fasting, among other things it emphasizes, like good exercises, sunshine, diet, "positive thinking," and fresh air.

The pioneer nature cure clinic that offers to fast, as therapeutic cure began operation in Edinburgh, and "the legendary **Tyringham** Hall in Buckinghamshire" reported having received patients who fasted their way out.

In the words of Tom Greenfield, the naturopath

"Fasting was used to treat heart disease, high blood pressure, obesity, digestive problems, allergies, headaches - pretty much everything."

The procedure could be anywhere from a day, two, three up to months, especially for **obese patients.** The government monitored practitioners until scientific medicine developed a better cure against the Nature cure in Britain.

Although therapeutic cure remains relevant in some therapeutic fasting centers in Germany, some hospitals still offer "fasting weeks" supported by health insurance programs for obesity.

Recall also that fasting holidays are available at specific centers and health resorts in countries like Hungary, the Czech Republic, and Austria.

Fasting is also in Germany partly because it's considered part of medical practice. On this note, a doctor could easily recommend fasting for patients. More recently, it has led to the concept of **intermittent fasting,** with millions trying the 5:2 fasting/diet plan **or** the intake of certain food/ drinks for a specified period.

In his suggestion, Greenfield maintained that,

"If people can do a one day fast for a minimum of twice a year - maybe one in spring and one in the autumn and setting aside a day they can rest, when they just drink water - this will help mitigate the toxic effects of daily living."

Generally, clinically supervised fasting has been a significant part of medical treatment over the years in Europe and has continued to gather momentum in America as alternative medicine.

And some medical experts have also agreed on fasting as the center of detoxification therapy, base on the principle that accumulated toxic is responsible for most ill-health conditions.

Fasting and insulin

Though every food adds insulin to the body, some count more than others; Eating the right food will reduce the insulin level, but total self-denial of food remains the best insulin reduction method and, by extension, disease prevention. Hence the need for periodic and intentional abstinence of rations called fasting.

One of the recent diet trends is the aggressive search for a so-called workable miracle diet for healing, thereby returning society to the ancient curative practices of dietary selection and, sometimes, outright fasting.

For many, fasting evokes starvation, which is wrong; fasting is a different ball game than **starving,** with fasting being voluntary and starvation an involuntary condition.

Spiritual reasons have always accounted for most fasting, but recent trends suggest that more people are fasting for healthy living purposes. It implies fasting is a part of our regular activities.

The word "Breakfast" is said to be a meal that "Breaks the all-night fast," suggesting that fasting is a daily activity.

C   2

Intermittent Fasting

Intermittent fasting refers to the reasonable practice of planned, periodic abstinence of food, ranging from 12hrs up to 36hrs, based on specified protocol. Exceptions like water, tea, bone broth, and coffee are allowed.

There's also an overnight fast identified as 12/12, regarded as a straightforward kind of intermittent fasting protocol.

Perhaps, you might understand intermittent fasting better when you see it as an eating pattern instead of a diet.

Intermittent fasting, it was said, began partially in the United States as a result of "a 2014 TEDx Talk-*Why fasting bolsters brain power*" by **Mark Mattson**, *a neuroscientist at Johns Hopkins Medicine*:[1]

Talking about intermittent fasting and its different versions, Mattson noted that 16:8 plan-16 hours a day fast, with an eight-hour meal window, seems the most patronized.

Adding:

"There have been no studies comparing the different intermittent fasting approaches in humans, … so all we can see is that several different [IF] approaches are better than three meals plus snacks every day."

Intermittent fasting affects your hormones

Worthy of note here is that fasting, while helping you drop weight, may affect your hormones because body fat helps the body store energy in calories.

And during fasting, the body quickly adjusts to reality by tapping from reserve energy that is accessible. Also, the nervous system activity changes with other essential hormones.

Find below some metabolic alteration that occurs while you fast:

Insulin intensities go up when you eat. But when fasting, it goes down by force, thereby facilitating the breaking down of fat.

The nervous system takes **norepinephrine (noradrenaline)** to the fat cells. And it enables the body to quickly burn fat into allowed **fatty acids (**used for strength).

Dependable research shows that alternate-day fast (3 to 12 weeks duration) and whole day fast (12 to 24 weeks duration) causes a reduction in weight and body fat; however, the possible long-term effect of intermittent fasting remains unknown.

Note also that fasting will change growth hormone: the "Human Growth Hormone- **HGH** level." This change may see the rise of this hormone up to five times higher.

Earlier knowledge had linked the HGH to faster fat burn, but more recent findings suggest that it could alert the brain to retain more energy, which could restrict weight loss, according to a trusted online source.

This happens when a little inhabitant of **agouti**-related protein –AgRP neurons are activated, making the HGH indirectly cause a rise in appetite, why reducing energy metabolism, it stated.

This means that while a short period of fasting could be significant for many bodily adjustments that enhance the breakup of fat, the rise in HGH levels could impact metabolism to stop continuous weight loss.

Doing exercise during intermittent fasting

While discussing the overall benefit of intermittent fasting as a dietary pattern, many persons were concerned about managing their hunger in the fasting period and doing their daily routine.

Prominent among these is the question related to intermittent fasting and exercise, especially regarding how safe it is to exercise while following this fasting diet pattern.

Experts have always advised that people should eat balanced meals before and after exercising. This is because food intake before a workout session gives the body strength to do any exercise; just as after the workout, food aid in muscle recovery and rebuilding.

Hence, a good meal is an integral part of realizing your fitness objective. During intermittent fasting, you should not take anything other than water, tea, or coffee: within the fasting window. And so, assuming you decide to exercise within this period of your fast, what do you do?And so, assuming you decide to exercise within this period of your fast, what do you do?

First, you have to be more careful and, if possible, avoid all forms of strenuous physical activity that, of course, requires much energy to accomplish. Otherwise, you may be exposing yourself to fatigue that can even lead to higher injury risk.

Some persons think that doing exercise during a fast is not useful, but few studies suggest that doing cardio on an unfilled stomach can assist in weight loss.

A finding published in *the Journal of Nutrition and Metabolism*[2] discovered that exercising while fasting can upsurge fat oxidation. The body, it said starts, breaking down stored fat immediately to produce the needed energy.

Obesity journal report of a 2017 study noted that controlled fasting periods are more effective compared to caloric counting in reducing kilos. However, a different study reported in *the Journal of the International Society of Sports Nutrition* did not see a change in the weight loss between persons who did exercise while fasting and those that ate a meal before a workout.

It would be best if you plan your exercise during a fast carefully. You must put the following into consideration if you're fasting and wish to workout:

Kind of exercise: If you're working out within the eating window, it will not be an issue; but in the fasting window, consider light activities walking, yoga, etc.

Exercise time and timing: It's always healthier to schedule your exercise after meals, but the best time to do this is usually in the morning: before breakfast. If you're working out within eating periods, think of "preworkout nutrition," usually taken 2 to 3 hours before the exercise; such a meal should be rich in "complex carbohydrates" like protein, whole-grain, and cereal.

As a rule, always remember that it's important to remain physically active while doing intermittent fasting. If you must exercise, make sure you're hydrated before, within, and after the exercise, with enough liquid.

Discussing the Myths of Fasting

We must learn how to separate facts about fasting from fiction handed down from generation to generation, otherwise referred to as myths. This is if we must understand the concept of fasting and what it's meant to achieve in our life.

Are you willing to practice intermittent fasting, or you're just considering the idea; perhaps you want to know more about fasting different from what you already know.

I will examine some facts you need to know about what constitutes fasting and what is not. Knowing these facts will help you engage in fasting the proper way and benefit from the numerous advantages that fasting offers. This includes weight reduction, stable energy, and reduced thirst that popularized the concept of intermittent fasting.

It will interest you to know that lots of untrue information are available about fasting, even as some are mere speculation. You may have heard people say:

"Fasting makes sluggish the metabolism process; you should not take water while fasting, or that fasting shrinks the muscles."

The above suggestions are all based on mere speculation, without any proven scientific support. As such, they are misplaced reliance on conservative knowledge.

When you understand the truth about fasting, you will marvel at the useful things it does towards improving the much desired healthy living.

It makes the body pulse on digestion that consumes much energy to fight **oxidative stress** and do things like cellular repairs for better health.

There's the 16/8 protocol for people who prefer to eat their entire daily intake within an eight-hour window.

The **OMAD** protocol means that you go with "One Meal per Day.

Another intermittent fasting protocol is the 5/2; this allows a five-day average food intake with two irregular fasting days weekly.

And finally, the **ADF: alternate-day fasting,** as the name implies, you alternate your fast daily.

Most people will go for intermittent fasting for lots of reasons, including but not limited to weight loss, do a burn-down of health, enhances longevity, and relevant cognitive abilities.

How exactly does this happen? *In simple terms, fasting tells the body to discontinue sugar smashing of sugar and start smashing fat-* a process known as **ketosis.** Hence, we can talk about the importance of the **keto diet,** as both fasting and keto diet helps the body burn fat, make ketones that ensure easy and regular energy to the body.

The myths

Now, let's look at the myths that seem to have surrounded the concept of fasting over time, especially now that you know what intermittent fasting is; these debunked myths tell you what intermittent fasting is not.

1. **Fasting will reduce metabolism-** No, fasting will not. The fear that fasting will cause you to breakdown fewer calories at rest-reducing the rate of resting metabolism that should give you more weight after fasting is not accurate.

When you're on a calorie-limiting diet (consuming daily 50 to 80% of food requirements in the body) over time, the body's metabolism recognizes these low-energy foods and adapts to them.

In the *American Journal of Clinical Nutrition* 2005 report, a study on nonobese persons that did the alternate-day fasting showed that regular metabolic rate is sustained for three weeks, even as they continue to burn more fat.

2. **Don't drink water when you're fasting-** No, you may require water. Specific religious fast like **Ramadan** assumes no-water fast is good for

wellbeing. However, fasting without water has a **diuretic effect** that may lead to problematic dehydration.

This explains why doctors observing patients on therapeutic fasting monitor fluid intake, plus electrolytes-sodium, potassium, and the likes that seems to reduce rapidly during fast.

So take water while fasting. If possible, support it with sodium and potassium, especially if you're fasting beyond 13 to 14hrs.

3. **You'll not add a muscle during fasting-** Though it may not be the right muscle builder, the amount of protein required for this is not entirely affected, as shown by recent research.

Apart from the fact that you do not need protein every hour of the day, the body has a way of retaining muscle during scarcity.

So apparently, when you're fasting, the body depends on fat rather than muscle for strength.

4. **Fasting will make you eat more after-** Rationally, one assumes that the attendant hunger that followed after fasting could make one want to take more food than necessary.

There is, however, no practical evidence to support this claim as **"libitum feeding"** in studies allows contributors to feed as required with many, losing weight still.

5. **Fasting is for all-** No, it's not. Despite the numerous benefits that intermittent fasting offers, there is a concern about a certain category of persons embarking on it.

This include:

- All pregnant women and nursing mothers

- Malnourished persons and,

- Children

This is because the danger involved in nutrient deficiency is better avoided than the required benefit from fasting.

Persons with high blood sugar should also be cautious about fasting. If possible, they should go with strict supervision to prevent **Hypoglycemia,** a dangerously low blood sugar level.

6. **Fasting drains energy**- Well, initially, it may seem so. But during intermittent fasting, the body will adapt to changes by using **Body fat,** a different energy source that is readily available.

7. **You will not focus if you're fasting**- On the contrary, intermittent fasting, unlike starvation, will not take you to that level of hunger that should make you lose focus.

Because the body cells get accustomed to it, your energy source diverts and equalizes the hunger hormones.

In addition to the small molecules known as **ketosis,** it activates the brain with perfect energy.

It's nice for us to do away with all this falsehood of information being spread about Fasting if we hope to get the real benefit accrued to those who do intermittent fasting**.**

8. **Fasting is Antisocial**- This also should not be the case since you're doing your intermittent fasting on choice, and not by force: to achieve a specific objective. So when you feel like you're antisocial while fasting, remember that you have an objective to accomplish. If not, you might be doing it the wrong way.

The program is meant to improve your health and, by extension, your lifespan here on earth, as such should not be seen as a punishment or the likes, your life and health are more important than anything else, and so nothing should deprive you of it.

9. **Women Can't Fast**- No reason has been given yet, but women seem more sensitive to hunger signals than men. Typically, if the body notices

that it's being starved, it quickly upgrades the hunger hormones, **leptin,** and **ghrelin** production.

If women encounter this feeling of unquenchable hunger because of not eating enough, it is said that what they're feeling is the above-stated hormones. This explains how a woman's body is designed to protect a potential fetus, at all time; including when they're not pregnant.

Particularly, women's negative energy balance accounts for the frequent hormonal changes in their bodies, not just the amount of food being consumed.

This negative energy balance can be because of:

- Little food consumed

- Poor feeding

- Excessive exercise

- Excessive stress

- Illness and chronic inflammation

- Lack of rest and recovery

Thus, combining the above is enough to put one into a negative energy balance and subsequently affect the hormones.

Things like preparing for a marathon while you nurture the flu; spending longer-hours at the gym without enough fruits and vegetables; together with intermittent fasting may be too hard on your body to cause this adverse effect.

I have seen both women and men who adopted a superman approach; they soon discover that they have taken more than they can swallow.

It's even worse if one is actively engaged in an incredibly stressful work life, with not-too good sleeping habits; some also add caffeine, and nicotine to the already weakened body, daily.

These things joined together will introduce excessive stress to the body that will eventually throw the hormones out of sync. This is true for all men and women; women are more subtle to stress.

Rewards Derived from Intermittent Fasting

It's indeed amazing to know that the brain, the body, and overall your health can benefit a lot from fasting. But I'm guessing that you're still somewhat confused about how fasting can do as much towards achieving all the things being talked about.

Perhaps, it's time to take a deep breath as I expose you to certain things you need to know about intermittent fasting; before you start omitting your meals.

Do you still remember that you were once told that breakfast is the most important food of the day? Research that reported the possible benefits of a.m. meals seems to have changed that narrative. Hence, the increasing number of persons embracing intermittent fasting, even though fasting is as old as humankind.

Recall that men were not sure of when the next meal would be available in the hunter-gatherer era.

Recall also that people are advised to fast to have **mental clarity and total health** in **Chinese medicine** and Ayurveda practices. At the same time, religious groups maintained the need to fast for divine benefits.

Advantages of intermittent fasting

Many lovers of this eating pattern have boasted of its numerous benefits, ranging from high energy and mental clarity to disease prevention; while also doing wonders in reducing body weight (weight loss).

It may not be out of place to say that intermittent fasting as a way of life has come to stay owing to the recent scientific evidence giving credence to its benefits to the human body in the area of:

- Inflammation decrease.

- Reduction of **cholesterol**, **Blood Pressure**, **Blood triglycerides**, and **LDL cholesterol**

- Body **Sugar level** control through balance insulin sensitivity.

- Excellent weight loss from a decrease in calorie consumption, with quick upward adjustment to resting energy outflow.

- Helps to improve **degenerative brain illness.**

- Reduces inflammation in the gut.

This being the case, I have to give my candid advice here. To anyone thinking of making intermittent fasting a lifestyle, just like you will do while changing your diet, it's beneficial to define what you intend to achieve from it.

Are you hoping to burn some fat and achieve a reasonable weight loss? You have to understand that being on a certain diet and lifestyle changes can help you achieve weight loss.

This knowledge will maximize intermittent fasting benefits if you decide to take it as a better option.

REDUCES CALORIES

Regardless of the fasting protocol that you might be observing, there's always a reduction in calories; unless you're messing up the meal skipping by overeating within the eating window.

Eating less frequently means taking-in fewer calories.

In some 2014 studies about intermittent fasting, bodyweight was reportedly reduced by 3 to 8% 3 to 24 weeks.

Credible sources have confirmed the rate at which weight loss occurs during intermittent fasting to be about 0.55-1.65 pounds, somewhere between 0.25 to 0.75kg in a week.

There is also a possible 4 to 7% decline in waist perimeter, showing a reduction in **belly fat.**

You should know that while you may not count calories while fasting, weight loss is a product of a total reduction in calories.

In her opinion, **Kathy McManus**, a *certified dietitian and the director of the Department of Nutrition at Harvard-affiliated Brigham and Women's Hospital,* noted:

"Fasting leads to lower levels of glucose (blood sugar). In response, the body uses fat instead of glucose as a source of energy, after turning the fat into ketones."

This shift from glucose to ketones as an energy source that healthily alters the body's chemistry.

Different experiment between intermittent fasting and regular calorie restraint indicates a similar result.

What this means is that fasting is a smooth way of reducing weight.

MUSCLE MAINTENANCE

Few facts suggest that fasting, rather than typical calorie restraint, helps a person maintain additional muscle. There is no evidence of this in recent studies.

HEALTHY EATING

Fasting ensures a healthy eating habit. This is because the most effective dietary pattern is the one that is easier and suitable for your ultimate goal. If you like fasting, it will have an obvious benefit in weight loss and overall health.

INCREASES METABOLISM

One surprise discovery is a rise in **purine** and **pyrimidine** levels, **even though researchers are yet to ascertain its connection with fasting.**

These chemicals are an indication of a rise in *"protein synthesis and gene expression."* This subsequently presupposes that fasting also makes cells to raise type and amount of proteins it needs to function.

An increase in purine and pyrimidine are an indication that the body could be improving the number of certain antioxidants. Researchers also noticed a considerable rise in certain antioxidants, like **ergothioneine** and **carnosine**.

Naturally, as one gets older, a certain quantity of metabolites reduces. These metabolites are **leucine, isoleucine**, and **ophthalmic** acid.

A study that uses rats shows that fasting enhanced these metabolites, thereby explaining how fasting could extend lifespan.

However, according to some scientists, the rise in antioxidants could be some survival instinct that comes during hunger, following high oxidative stress levels that the body often passes through. By manufacturing antioxidants, it could aid against potential damage that may take place by free die-hards.

General negative side effects?

Prolonged fasting reportedly causes issues, such as **moodiness, high-stress** intensities, **disordered sleep**, and **headaches**. It would help if you always understood your body signals, so you don't get caught up in an unpleasant situation that is self-inflicted.

Know when you're feeling like fainting, dizzy, nauseous, or shaky. It's better to disrupt your fasting temporarily than get yourself into trouble against the doctor's advice.

It could also contribute to what is described as "*forming a restrictionbingeing cycle*" that is atypical with calorie-limiting diets. This is so because some persons may naturally want to consume more if they think that they're missing out somehow, leading to **overeating** or **bingeing** when the time to eat arises.

This will cause an individual to add more weight, making nonsense of the entire fasting process negatively.

Intermittent fasting may also put a dent in your social life, mostly if you're adhering to it regularly for an extended period. Imagine abstaining in a brunch festivity because you don't want to alter the protocol. My opinion here is that it's a battle between your health and your social life.

C   3

Fasting for weight loss

While weight loss is achieved through different unique weight management programs, intermittent fasting seems to be gaining more relevance in recent times; as a weight loss program.

No wonder most persons will tell you that it's just a weight-loss activity, but it's much more than that.

A short period fast will make you eat lesser calories; that should translate to weight loss eventually.

Fasting plays a vital role in altering possibility factors for certain health conditions such as diabetes and cardiovascular disease. This is because fasting regularizes high blood sugar and cholesterol level.

Succeeding with intermittent fasting for weight loss

If you want to carry out intermittent fasting and derived its benefits successfully, you must realize the importance of the following:

1. **The Quality of food-** The nature of food being consumed during the fasting period is very significant; majorly, whole and single-ingredient meals work better.

2. *Calories- Be conscious of calories at all times by not overeating during the mealtime window while fasting, so you don't ignorantly replace the calories that you're trying to reduce.[2]*

3. *Consistency- As obtainable in other weight loss programs, you're expected to regularly stick to it a little longer for a more efficient outcome.*

4. *Endurance-* *It takes some practice for the body to adjust to the fasting protocol you're in, so you have to be patient.*

A recent article[3] that fasting might not be suitable for everybody though it's beneficial to many.

Can fasting promote weight loss?

Even though much research has proven that fasting can significantly play a major role in promoting weight loss, researchers have also said that it might not be so for all persons.

Notable diet protocols like the 12hrs or 16hrs fasting periods, even the 24hrs fast, are not automatically better than other weight-loss programs, making lesser your daily calorie intake inclusive.

A report published recently indicates that people with obesity that fasted intermittently for a year lost a little more weight than those who did dieting in the usual way. However, the results did not show statistical importance.[4]

The perimeter of fasting should be how it blends with a lifestyle rather than its physical effects.

For instance, the report revealed that those who fasted were more eager to abandon their weight-loss pursuit than those who regularly dieted for weight loss, like counting calories.

With these, they opined that fasting might be more challenging to sustain in the long run.

Fasting for Type 2 Diabetes

It sees experts are somewhat skeptical on claims that intermittent fasting could inverse type 2 diabetes. A recent study of three-male suggests that random fasting could inverse type 2 diabetes.

A particular researcher noted that occasional fasting could inverse type 2 diabetes, though others could not ascertain this yet.

The sampled men with type 2 diabetes halted insulin treatment after they fasted, though experts warn that such practice is risky without relevant medical supervision.

As published recently,[5] the three men whose age ranges from 40 to 67 had tried occasional fasting for about ten months, with the result showing that they all stopped insulin treatment a month after. A particular man among the studied was able to halt insulin medication just after five days of fasting.

What this study implies is that:

" a dietary intervention-therapeutic fasting-has the potential to completely reverse type 2 diabetes, even when somebody has suffered from the disease for over 25 years."

This definitely should change how we see the disease, **Dr. Jason Fung**, *the author of the study and director of the Intensive Dietary Management Program*, stated.

Fung's claim of type 2 diabetes being reversible through fasting is contrary to a few diabetes experts who commented on this.

Commenting on the tricky nature of diabetes, **Dr. Matthew Freeby**, *the director of the Gonda Diabetes Center, Los Angeles,* noted:

"It's potentially dangerous to tell patients their diabetes has been reversed because one is always at risk for progression, even if not being treated by medication."

Freeby, an associate director of diabetes clinical programs at the David Geffen UCLA School of Medicine, knows the kind of feeling that could follow if a diabetes patient gets to hear this.

The chief medical officer at the Joslin Diabetes Center, Massachusetts, **Dr. Robert Gabbay,** was of the same view as Freeby:

"We don't think of reversing it, but more that it is in remission. Still need to screen for complications as far as we know,"

He added.

What's the issue with diabetes

According to a report by the Center for Disease Control and Prevention, of about 30 million persons in the United States already living with diabetes, 90 to 95% are down with type 2 diabetes.

Explaining why the cells of a type 2 diabetes' patient do not usually respond to the insulin that aids in blood sugar control, **Lauri Wright**, **PhD**. and *an assistant professor of public health at the University of South Florida,* says:

> *"When we eat foods containing carbohydrates (pieces of bread, cereals, pasta, fruits, starchy vegetables, dairy), the body digests the carbohydrates into single sugars. The pancreas simultaneously receives a signal to release insulin. Insulin is released into the bloodstream and*
> *acts as a key to unlock the cells, allowing the single sugars to enter the cells and provide energy."*

She added that:

> *"Without enough functioning insulin, as we see in type 2 diabetes, some of the single sugars build up in the cell and aren't able to provide cells with energy."*

I guess you still remember that high blood sugar levels are hazardous to the body as it could cause many health issues, including kidney problems, heart issues, vision loss, etc.

And so, Type 2 diabetes could be handled with healthy eating and exercise, though a patient may need an insulin injection to aid his or her blood sugar levels.

Research findings

Still, in Fung's study, the pattern of the three men who started intermittent fasting to ascertain its possible effect on their diabetes are as follows:

Of the men, two fasted every second day, 24 hours each day, while one fasted for three days per week. The procedure included intake of lowcalorie drinks like water, coffee, tea, and broth, during fasting; also allowed is a nighttime low-calorie meal.

> *"The thing that surprised me most was how quickly patients got better,"*

Fung said, adding:

> *"Even after 25 years of diabetes, the maximum time it took to get off insulin was 18 days. All three patients improved their diabetes to the point that they no longer required insulin, and it only took from 5 to 18 days in this study."*

As you have seen, this is indeed the wonder of intermittent fasting on diabetes; so now that you've known, perhaps it's time to tell a friend about intermittent fasting and have them say thank you sometime in the future.

Though there is a need for an elaborate study on this, Fung advised.

Cautions

Experts all agreed on the need for caution when explaining the outcome of such an anecdotal examination.

Raquel Pereira, *a certified dietitian specializing in diabetes*, thinking different when he said:

> *"To many people with diabetes, such a study conclusion can be perceived as insulting."*

Adding that lots of:

> *"People with diabetes already suffer from the disease prognosis, complications, and limitations.*
> *Imagine hearing that the way that they can manage such disease is to then deprive themselves of nutritious foods, which provide health benefits as well as energy and pleasure."*

While advising on the way forward, she urged:

> *"As researchers, we must invest our efforts into solutions that are more attainable and have a more positive health impact for the vast majority of people with diabetes."*

In her opinion, fasting for people with diabetes could be somewhat harmful and need strict medical supervision; according to her, the study on fasting is negligible and requires a more elaborate and better-controlled examination to ascertain the actual state of things.

She also identified *"Disordered eating patterns"* as common in diabetes. As such, the long-term consequences of fasting may make one feel low energy, low reflexes, poor mental concentration, reduced immunity, headaches, resulting in a low quality of life and productivity.

Perhaps, fasting will not always have an affirmative effect on persons with diabetes; because on insulin, for instance, fasting can cause the diabetic patient **hypoglycemia**. This isn't good because people should eat the usual way when they resume eating after a fast.

Diabetic experts who do not want people to rely much on the above study all agreed that it should be *"such that gives us clues for further research"* before it can be recommended generally.

Fasting for a Younger Person

Quickly, let me begin here by letting you know that *"The fasting diet can keep you young,"* according to a Harvard University study that tries to explain how fasting plans like the 5:2 helps our cells from aging.

It found that:

Intermittent fasting protects a cell section, which significantly influences aging, makes one healthier, and elongates lifespan.

Fasting helps section of the cell: in the mitochondria- a state that stops aging.

The newest finding of how the anti-aging impact may help researchers get therapies that should stop age-related infections, the researchers stated, in an article published recently by **Natalie Rahhal**.[6]

What did Harvard Researchers say precisely about this? They noted that temporarily limiting diet protects the mitochondria – a useful section of the cell from aging in homeostasis.

This implies that intermittent fasting will keep your body very much younger while extending your lifespan and overall health.

These may be some of the reasons for the recent hype that has characterized fasting, and between those for and those against it, for weight loss and productivity improvement.

For many, while the argument had continued without a shift from either side, the Harvard study that explains how intermittent fasting may delay aging at a cellular level seems to have given more credence and boosted the morale of those who may want to fast.

No wonder it's seen as the "new juice" lately. Even celebrities such as **Benedict Cumber batch**, **Beyonce**, Silicon Valley executives reportedly extolled the merits of the 5:2 diet.

Recall that *Newcastle University's* research recently gave credit to the **mitochondria's** crucial function in our body cell on aging.

Mitochondria smash carbohydrates and fatty acids and release energy to the cell; hence, they're called the "powerhouses" of body cells.

The **Mitochondria** are in two states, and at any time the two states are alternating appropriately, we say they're in homeostasis.

Adding to this, **Dr. William Mair**, *a researcher and associate professor of genetics and complex diseases at the Harvard T.H. Chan School of Public Health,* said:

"By eating in the day, you're not challenging the mitochondria at night, when they're supposed to be doing other things…, But we have many unanswered questions."

From the information available, the mitochondria stay in homeostasis better if an organism, e.g., a **nematode worm**: *"has an intermittently restricted diet"* and still be able to swing as usual from one state to another. This, researchers say, is the key to longevity- improving the impact of intermittent fasting.

They added that intermittent fasting aid in coordinating mitochondria activities with **peroxisomes** and other sections of a cell, having an antioxidant impact; that should contribute to longevity.

These newest discoveries are the principal understanding of how fasting operates at a cellular level and could help in discovering therapies expected to benefit lifespan elongation and the younger body.

C 4

Fasting for Heart Health

How accurate is the saying that observing a fasting plan can lower one's risk of heart disease?

Possibly, investigators are not convinced about this. However, some fasting that involves the strict restriction of food and drinks within a specified period seems to have the potential to improve certain risk factors related to heart health.

It appears somewhat difficult to ascertain the exact effect frequent fasting has on human heart health, owing to the diverse reasons why lots of people fast, though majorly for health or religious purposes.

We only have to depend on certain studies that say people who adhere to a fasting diet could show better heart fitness than others who do not. There's a belief that a healthy heart is associated with how the body metabolizes cholesterol and sugar within the period.

Frequent fasting is said to lower **low-density lipoprotein**-"faulty" cholesterol while improving how the body metabolizes sugar. For this reason, it works well on weight loss and early diabetes. Both of which are risk factors for heart problems.

Fasting has good heart health potential, but additional examination is needed to ascertain how regular fasting can make-less heart disease risk. As I have often stated, *"If you're considering regular fasting, talk to your doctor"* first.

Recall that the *New England Journal of Medicine,* on its page,[7] recently made public an *"authoritative review of research on intermittent fasting and its potential for reducing a great many health risks,"* that included manifold **sclerosis**, intestinal disorders, and a variety of cancers.

Johns Hopkins Mark Mattson, one of the study's co-leads, exposed the useful benefits of fasting to heart health. According to him, fasting reduces the risk factors of **HDL** and **LDL**-good and bad cholesterol levels, blood pressure, resting heart rate; also triglycerides, insulin, glucose, and insulin resistance-metabolic syndrome.

"Intermittent fasting enables overweight people to lose weight and improve many different health indicators, including glucose regulation, cardiovascular risk factors, and inflammation."

Mattson noted.

You will discover that insulin resistance usually advances to pre-diabetes, before normal diabetes, high blood pressure, and then **atherosclerosis**, the freezing of the arteries.

Let me quickly add here that according to information on her website,[8] the *American Heart Association* wrote on two examinations that intermittent fasting-*"is associated with lower rates of heart failure and a longer life span."*

Presenting the preliminary findings at the **AHA** conference, **epidemiologist Benjamin Horne** hinted that the research outcome shows a *"more profound effect (on heart health) than we anticipated."*

Medical professionals still request additional studies towards ascertaining its possible short and long-term gains with potential adverse effects, if any.

The director of Preventive Cardiovascular Medicine at the University of Miami Miller School of Medicine, **Carl E. Orringer,** will not recommend intermittent fasting to his patients with heart issues. Although he did not dispute the knowledge in the New England Journal of Medicine's report, he expressed concerns about applicability in reality with three statements:

●It's hard to apply, with culturally ingrained mealtimes schedules.

●It could cause temporary hunger, tetchiness, and issues of concentration.

●Doctors are untrained for such prescriptions.

In his words:

> *"I have my doubts about how many patients will actually get access to the counseling and followup that will be needed to maximize the suggested benefits."*

Explaining further, Mattson observed that beginners initially might *"be hungry and irritable during the time when they had previously been eating,"* adding that:

> *"within two to four weeks, their energy-regulating neuroendocrine systems and hunger-regulating circuits in their brains will adapt, and they will no longer be hungry during the fasting period."*

By eating a meal, **leptin**-(hormone) release into the bloodstream. *"Leptin acts on the **hypothalamus**,"* and thus,

> *"sends signals to higher brain centers, which give you the 'I'm full' feeling; on the other hand when you have not eaten anything for a long time, a hormone called ghrelin is released instead. Ghrelin acts on the hypothalamus to trigger the 'I'm hungry' feeling."*

He concluded.

Who Should Not Fast

The majority of the research done so far on intermittent fasting has centered on men, and results could not automatically be associated with women.

It's so because women have a more sophisticated system of hormones. Relevant researches indicate that intermittent fasting may result in "hormone imbalance" and asymmetrical periods in women.

Pregnant, breastfeeding, underweight, and persons with histories of ingestion disorders; diabetes patients, blood-sugar control issues, adrenal fatigue, severe stress, and certain medical conditions, are all persons who should ask their doctor first before fasting.

Assuming you do exercise six days per week, intermittent fasting is not for you; unless your gene is peculiar enough to adapt to the possibility of overtraining.

In addition to this, persons with final-stage liver disease should also stay away from fasting.

Is intermittent fasting safe for older adults?

Perhaps, you could try learning the risks, if any, before adopting this experimental eating pattern. For now, there's no such evidence that says older adults should not fast; instead, we may concentrate on how intermittent fasting affects the health of older adults. **Possible risks**

So far, researches have concentrated only on minor groups of young or middle-aged adults; but knowing that intermittent fasting could be risky in certain conditions, especially if you're a tiny-body body fellow.

It's possible that you'd be concerned that you could let-go too much weight that can interfere with your bones, immune system, etc.

"People who need to take their medications with food — to avoid nausea or stomach irritation — may not do well with fasting. Also, people who take heart or blood pressure medications may be more likely to suffer dangerous imbalances in potassium and sodium when they're fasting."

Dr. Suzanne Salamon, *the associate chief of gerontology at Harvardaffiliated Beth Israel Deaconess Medical Center*, had warned. Intermittent fasting, as stated earlier in this book, maybe dangerous for diabetes' patient that need food at definite times or are on medication that impacts blood sugar.

But if you think, against all odds, you want to try this fasting trend, experts advised that those with pre-medical conditions like diabetes and heart disease should discuss it with their doctor before commencement.

Again, you could gradually reduce the time window for meals so that your body can naturally adapt to it as you observe your progress.

According to **Dr. Alexander Soukas,** an *endocrinologist and molecular geneticist with Harvard-affiliated Massachusetts General Hospital, y*ou must continue your drugs if you decide to fast in-between your routine medical period. This is because medicines do not affect your fasting with calorie-free fluids like water and black coffee.

If your medication requires eating a meal, you can always consider a modified fasting plan.

What healthy women need to know on intermittent fasting

It's unnecessary to take post-dinner snacks after having a balanced meal because it's not the right thing to do while fasting; instead, you should take a full glass cup of water. Even if you're working within that hour, it has a way of making you feel mentally proud.

Again, starting your day with water is an excellent way to begin: this is the practice of drinking water, first thing in the morning before any other thing like coffee or a full meal. It has proven to do excellently well in the body health-wise. Hence, the need to consider it as a useful drill.

Early morning exercise might be suitable while you're on this diet plan, as you're very likely to feel weak each time you try to; unless you're extraordinarily endowed with more energy.

In her view, **Torey Armul**, M.S., R.D., speaking for the *Academy of Nutrition and Dietetics*, on being super active while on a diet plan:

"Your muscles need fuel to function properly, and carbohydrates are the most efficient source of muscle fuel. Your body can store carbohydrates, but only for a few hours at a time. That's why you're hungry when you wake up in the morning, and why you 'hit the wall' during morning workouts if you haven't eaten yet,"

She noted.

Kind of Fast and Best Practices

Let's examine how you can conveniently do intermittent fasting (IF) no matter how you want to fast. To call it **intermittent fasting**, it should be such that you determine the days you'll fast and the calorie allowances. **Major ways to effectively do intermittent fasting**

It's all about partially abstaining from your meal, for a specified period, before resuming regular eating again. Everyone should have peculiar experiences about intermittent fasting because of inherent differences in individual eating lifestyles, so do well to choose what's best for you.

12 HOURS A DAY FASTING

The fasting plan or protocol rules are simple; you specify when to eat and when not to within a 12-hour fasting window each day.

This kind of intermittent fasting is a better option for starters because the fasting window is somewhat small, as the most time of the fast will be during sleep, with a similar number of calorie consumption each day.

The easiest method of doing a 12-hour fast is to assign your sleeping period to the fasting window.

For example, a 12 hours fasting is assigning 6.pm. to 6.am, daily for fasting, and after 6 a.m till 6 p.m for the food eating window.

16-HOURS FASTING

This is assigning 16 hours for fasting daily. Maintaining a food consumption window of 8 hours is mathematically called the "16:8 method" or the **Leangains** protocol.

THE 16/8 METHOD

	DAY 1	DAY 2	DAY 3	DAY 4	DAY 5	DAY 6	DAY 7
Midnight 4 AM 8 AM	FAST	FAST	FAST	FAST	FAST	FAST	FAST
12 PM	First meal	First meal	First meal	First meal	First meal	First meal	First meal
4 PM	Last meal by 8pm	Last meal by 8pm	Last meal by 8pm	Last meal by 8pm	Last meal by 8pm	Last meal by 8pm	Last meal by 8pm
8 PM Midnight	FAST	FAST	FAST	FAST	FAST	FAST	FAST

With this 16:8 diet, you naturally abstain from food for 16 hrs daily; other diets focus on strong rules and regulations, but the 16:8 method is a more flexible **TRF** model- time-restricted feeding.

Popularized by fitness specialist **Martin Berkhan**, you may drink water, and zero-calorie drinks within the fasting, to reduce hunger feel.

It's easier to adapt to, though some persons may find it demanding to avoid a meal for that long-16 hours. Again, consuming more snacks and related junk foods within the 8-hour window will not give you the expected benefits of the 16:8 fasting.

So try eating a balanced diet that should comprise of fruits, whole grains, vegetables, protein, and healthy fats for optimum health benefits.

This method is okay for people that completed the 12hrs fast without the required outcome; some say women doing this method should fast for 14 hours.

A more recent study did suggest that the 16:8 method does not damage gains in muscle or energy in women doing resistance training.[9]

With this, you will finish your evening meal by 8 p.m., omit breakfast the following day, and waiting until noon for another meal.

2-DAYS PER WEEK FASTING

Also known as the 5:2 diets required you to eat a good number of healthy food for 5-days and fast for the remaining 2-days of the week, **Michael Mosley**, a British journalist, popularized it.

THE 5:2 DIET

DAY 1	DAY 2	DAY 3	DAY 4	DAY 5	DAY 6	DAY 7
Eats normally	Women: 500 calories Men: 600 calories	Eats normally	Eats normally	Women: 500 calories Men: 600 calories	Eats normally	Eats normally

It is left for you to decide the fasting days within the week; you may fast Mondays and Thursdays and then eat normally on other days. But it would be best if you keep at least a day window in-between fasting days.

There's limited research on fast diet as it's often called, but a report of 107 weighty or obese women shows that twice a week calorie restriction and continuous restriction led to similar weight loss, based on a report.[10]

While also reducing insulin levels and improving insulin sensitivity on the participants.

For those who may consume up to 2,000 calories daily, this fasting method reduces the daily calorie intake to 500 for women and 600 for men within the two days of the week, which may not be easy for some persons, according to an article.[11]

4. ALTERNATE DAY FASTING

This method has many variations that include fasting every other day, allowing about 500 calories during the fast. While some people avoid completely solid foods on fasting days, others could allow up to 500 calories on fasting days and eating as much as they want on meal days.

Alternate day

| Eats normally | 24-hour fast OR Eat only a few hundred calories | Eats normally | 24-hour fast OR Eat only a few hundred calories | Eats normally | 24-hour fast OR Eat only a few hundred calories | Eats normally |

Alternate-day fast appears to be an extreme kind of intermittent fasting and may be hard for beginners; equally, persons with certain medical conditions. Also, it's somewhat difficult to sustain long term fasting.

24-HOUR WEEKLY FASTING

If you're doing a 24-hour fast, you may take teas and other calorie-free fluids. Also refers to "Eat Stop Eat."

It's an unusual approach to intermittent fasting made popular by the author of the book "Eat Stop Eat," **Brad Pilon**.

You create a day or two non-consecutive days each week for food abstinence that lasts for a 24-hour-period; while you eat normally other days of the week, overindulgence is not optional. But this will need too much willpower to overcome and often leads to bingeing.

In all, always remember to feed on a nutritious diet while you fast

. MEAL SKIPPING

This is a flexible way of doing intermittent fasting, convenient for beginners: you skip meals intentionally. You have to decide the meal to miss considering time restraints or the rate of hunger. It's also useful to eat healthy foods when you take each meal.

SPONTANEOUS MEAL SKIPPING

	DAY 1	DAY 2	DAY 3	DAY 4	DAY 5	DAY 6	DAY 7
	Breakfast	Skipped Meal	Breakfast	Breakfast	Breakfast	Breakfast	Breakfast
	Lunch	Lunch	Lunch	Lunch	Lunch	Lunch	Lunch
	Dinner	Dinner	Dinner	Dinner	Skipped Meal	Dinner	Dinner

It's best if you want to monitor and respond to your body's hunger indications. This practically requires you to eat when you're hungry and skip when you're not, though more natural for most people than the other fasting methods.

THE WARRIOR DIET

The Warrior Diet is more of an extreme kind of intermittent fasting.

This plan allows you to eat very small, mainly a few portions of uncooked fruit and vegetables: within a 20-hour fasting window, with a big meal at night; this eating window occurs within 4 hours: made popular by **Ori Hofmekler,** a fitness expert.

The food choices are related to those of the paleo diet that emphasized whole and unprocessed foods.

THE WARRIOR DIET

	DAY 1	DAY 2	DAY 3	DAY 4	DAY 5	DAY 6	DAY 7
Midnight 4 AM 8 AM 12 PM	Eating only small amounts of vegetables and fruits	Eating only small amounts of vegetables and fruits	Eating only small amounts of vegetables and fruits	Eating only small amounts of vegetables and fruits	Eating only small amounts of vegetables and fruits	Eating only small amounts of vegetables and fruits	Eating only small amounts of vegetables and fruits
4 PM	Large meal	Large meal	Large meal	Large meal	Large meal	Large meal	Large meal
8 PM Midnight							

Experts say this one should be good for people that have tried other kinds of intermittent fasting already.

Proponents of the Warrior Diet assert that humans are nocturnal eaters, naturally; and as such, eating at night makes the body to absorb nutrients base on its day by day rhythms.

Take enough healthy fruits and vegetables, protein, and even carbohydrates during the 4-hour eating time.

This method is also challenging to maintain strict guidelines on eating in the long term; some persons will struggle to eat a big meal before bedtime.

Not eating enough nutrients like fiber could make-high the risk of cancer, experts warn.

And finally, intermittent fasting is a weight loss program. It works for many but will not work for all persons. Some persons say it may not be as useful to women as it is to men.

C   5
Longer Period and Extended fasting

48 hours fasting Though the short-duration fasting seems to be more popular and embraced by many, perhaps, they're already accustomed to it historically; some persons will still choose the fasting window that is a little longer than the short-period fast.

48-hour fast appears to be the longest duration done by those doing intermittent fasting. While you may be considering the possible benefit of this long period of fasting, it's also good that you think about its drawbacks.

Let me take you through the process involved in a more extended period of fasting and other things you need to know.

How to start a 48-hour fast

The concept of 48-hrs fasting is just straight and simple; you deny yourself food for two days. One usual way to accomplish this is to end eating after dinner on "a starting day" and continue eating again on the third, at dinnertime.

Well, against popular opinion, you may still consume no-calorie fluids, like water, black coffee, and so on, within the fasting period.

It's very helpful to hydrate your body with enough fluids to avoid dehydration that is a major factor that could cause likely complications on longer fasts.

When you're through with your fasting, experts advised that you gradually reestablish your normal eating style; so you don't overstimulate your gut; doing the contrary may cause diarrhea, bloating, and nausea.[12]

You might start eating after the fast with a light snack, e.g., one or two handfuls of almonds, and then you can wait for an hour or two for a little meal.

Within the non-fasting days, your normal eating pattern should be adhered to; while ensuring that you refrain from overindulging high-calorie content foods.

Usually, this fast is done once or twice a month, and not once or twice per week, as promoted by certain fasting proponents. A 48-hour fast that is well-spaced out will offer more health benefits, experts say.

Note also that this kind of fasting is not encouraged for all persons, and before you start considering the 48-hrs fast, you have to try shorter fasts, possibly the alternate-day fast, with no issue at all, before undertaking the 2-day term. The shorter fast will help you fathom how your body will respond to such a long period of no-food

Health benefits of 48-hour fasting

Although I have stated much about the health benefits accrued to those who venture into intermittent fasting, certain research focused specifically on the longer period fasting; feasibly defined as "prolonged fasting" focusing on fasting lasting more than 24 hours, shows the following results:

MAY SLOW CELL AGING

Cellular repair is the body's regular way of replacing its cells that protect the body from diseases, even delay tissue aging.

These two functions of improving cellular repair and delaying tissue aging positively impact overall longevity, although these findings rely on animals as samples.

More important is the findings that 48-hour fasting could improve cellular repair faster than other kinds of fasting plans.

Momentary inflammation is a normal way the immune system shows its response; however, more severe inflammation may have serious health effects like cancer, rheumatoid arthritis, and heart disease.[13]

According to an article,[14] fasting for a duration that is more than 24 hours can significantly lower inflammation; through reduced oxidative stress in the body's cells).

ENHANCES INSULIN SENSITIVITY AND BLOOD SUGAR LEVELS:

I guess you already know what fasting does to insulin in the body. However, reports show that a fast of longer than 24hrs works better on glycogen (the storage form of carbs). This is because it lowers the insulin level to allow the body to break down fat as energy[25].

Fasting longer than 24 hrs can also add additional benefit to blood sugar control than those seen in a shorter fast.[15]

WEIGHT LOSS:

While no study yet on the 48-hour fast, but just like other fasting protocols, this kind of fasting will result in a significant weight loss, as long as you don't overcompensate for the lost calories when you start eating. **Disadvantages of 48-hour fasting**

As you may have guessed, this longer fasting duration is not suitable for everybody, as the more the duration of a fast, the higher the risk potentials. If you think you're unfit within a fasting period, it is better to halt the fasting immediately and resume something in the future than get yourself in trouble.

Hunger and dizziness: The major drawback of 48hrs fasting is extreme hunger. Although it calms down after some time, it's still a source of concern.

Other disadvantages include exhaustion, sluggishness, and interference with social eating. Conclusively, it is not for those with special health conditions.

24 Hours fasting

What happens if you deny yourself food for a day or so? I might not provide you with a straight answer, but we all know the complex outcome a 24-hour fast could turn the body into. Let's examine what happens to the body when a day or so passes without any ingestion.

What happens in the body during fasting?

Whether you're fasting or not you, need energy in the body. This energy's primary source is a sugar known as glucose- mainly obtained from carbohydrate-rich foods like grains, fruits, dairy products, some vegetables, beans, etc.

Both the liver and the muscles save this glucose and send it to the bloodstream anytime the body requires it.

But within the fasting, these regular activities of the body change; fasting for about 8hrs will make the liver use up the stored glucose. Subsequently, the body begins **gluconeogenesis,** a process suggesting that the body has transited into a fasting mode.

Research indicates that gluconeogenesis helps the body to raise the number of calories burnt by the body.[16] With no new carbohydrates entering the body, it manufactures its energy source using mainly fat.

As this process continues, the body uses up these fat (energy sources) as well. If you do not eat within this period, the body will move from fasting mode to more serious starvation mode.

At this juncture, metabolism slows down while the body starts breaking down muscle tissue for energy.

Though it's a known concept in dieting culture, the real starvation mode can only happen after many consecutive days or weeks without any food.

So, if you're doing a day fasting, it's generally safe unless you consider other health conditions.

36 Hours fasting

Fasting for 36hrs is more like doing Alternate-Day fasting (ADF), researchers are still learning more about the long duration of fast, but more persons are concerned about the effect of this longer fast on their health.

A recent study focusing on alternate-day fasting discovered that it reduces belly fat and inflammation to a great extent. But experts argued that an extreme diet is required before one does this kind of fasting.

Explaining what she knows about this fast, a *bariatric endocrinologist at the Northwestern Medicine Metabolic Health and Surgical Weight Loss Center at Delnor Hospital in Illinois,* **Dr. Elizabeth Lowden,** noted that:

"Alternate-day fasting tends to include both regular food intake alternating with full fasting, meaning no food intake at all, or a significantly reduced intake of about 500 calories".

This study on the effects of strict ADF in people, as published by *the journal Cell Metabolism, Reported that:*

"Strict ADF is one of the most extreme diet interventions, and it has not been sufficiently investigated within randomized controlled trials."

This is according to the study author and *professor of the Institute of Molecular Biosciences at the Karl-Franzens University of Graz in Austria,* **Frank Madeo.**[17]

He added that the study examined a wide range of markers to ascertain the effects of the diet. In his words

"We aimed to explore a broad range of parameters, from physiological to molecular measures, … If ADF and other dietary interventions differ in their physiological and molecular effects, complex studies are needed in humans that compare different diets."

The study itself is a randomized controlled trial of 60 participants who did this for four weeks. The healthy and unhealthy persons were randomly divided into either ADF or a control group; another group of 30 that has completed ADF for 6 months before now were also studied.

The second group aims to know the effect ADF has on those with fasting experience and those without; identifying a long-term danger.

The ADF group did experience many advantages at the end that enhances a longer life span. From reduced belly fat to overall weight, lower cholesterol, etc.

Dry fasting

You have learned a lot about intermittent fasting and how to go about it; you have also learned that some fasting protocol will allow fluid intake within the fasting window while others will not. If your fasting protocol restricts both food and fluid intake, you're undergoing **dry fasting.**

Many persons talk about dry fasting as having more of a spiritual benefit than other forms of fasting; that is why it's more popular among many religious groups around the world.

An outstanding instance of this kind of fasting is the month-long Ramadan fast done by the Muslims within their holy month of Ramadan, from sunrise to sunset. However, water is acceptable at a certain period.

Dry or absolute fasting, as it's often called, can be incorporated in any of the intermittent fasting plans like the 16/8 fasting plan. Dry fasting experts say it is very dangerous because of the higher risk of dehydration and related complications, as against other fasting forms.

Though there's very little research on dry fasting, some supposed benefits and possible side effects will be examined below.

Those who have successfully carried out this fast have all maintained that they noticed the following:

1. A reduction in their weight (**weight loss**).

2. Better **immune system-** There's also a belief that this kind of fasting improves the immune system functions.

3. Reduced inflammation.

4. Cell regeneration.

5. Helping the skin with rapid wound healing

6. Diverse Spiritual benefits, as claimed by thousands of religious faithful, including more intense gratitude, more faith, better awareness, and

opportunity for a more acceptable prayer, being the most extreme form of self-denial.

Possible Side effects

1. There's a possibility of increased and persistent hunger since no fluid is taken.

2. Tiredness and irritability are very likely.

3. Headaches and poor focus (lack of concentration)

4. Reduced urination- This is a sure sign of dehydration, especially if your urine is darkish and smelly.

All this may lead to complications like **Urinary** and **kidney Issues, Nutrient Deficiencies, Fainting, Eating disorders,** among others.

C   6

Water fasting

Water fasting is a kind of fast that one can do by restricting everything but water. It's a speedy way to lose weight; if you're doing water fasting, you're not expected to eat anything other than water. Most water fasts are usually between 24 to 72hrs; anything longer, without a doctor's advice, is highly risky.

Major purposes people go for water fasting include losing weight, detoxification, other health benefits, being ready for a medical procedure (**Pediatric anesthetic**), and spiritual reason.

Pediatric anesthetic

According to Pediatric anesthetic recommendations for the management of **preoperative** fasting, two hours is adjudged okay. This old-style two hours clear fluid fasting period is advised to reduce the danger of **pulmonary aspiration.**

It appears that a relaxed, clear fluid fasting system does not affect pulmonary aspiration, especially on those who aspirate, though not usually severe or lasting for a long time.

According to the knowledge available, two-hour clear fasting means 6 to 7 hours of the actual fasting period, with many studies suggesting up to 15 hours. Generally, fasting for prolonged periods upsurges thirst and irritability that is detrimental to the human **physiological** and **metabolic** process.

But with a one-hour clear fluid system, no amplified risk of pulmonary aspiration was observed. Studies also show that the stomach is empty, even as the occurrence of things like nausea and vomiting, hunger, thirst, and anxiety is reduced. This is if you allow a patient to take fluid a little time before surgery.

Benefits of water fasting

Studies have linked water fasting to many health benefits, among which are:

CAN ENHANCE AUTOPHAGY

When aged, *"parts of your cells are broken down and recycled,"* a process known as Autophagy has occurred; this process, studies suggests, helps protect against infections like heart disease, cancer, and Alzheimer's.[18]

Autophagy prevents damaged parts of one's cells from accumulating, contributing to cancer risk factors: by not allowing cancer cells to grow from growing as contained in a report.[19]

MAY LOWER BLOOD PRESSURE

Extended and medically supervised water fast can help people with HBPhigh blood pressure. This is according to a related report that saw an average drop in blood pressure level to 20 mmHg for systolic -the upper value, and 7 mmHg for diastolic -the lower value. Researchers say it is significant. However, no human studies have examined the relationship between short-term water fasts and longer fasts between 24 to 72 hours on blood pressure.

CAN ENHANCE INSULIN AND LEPTIN SENSITIVITY

Insulin and leptin are two useful hormones that say a lot about the body's metabolism; while insulin stores the body's nutrients from the bloodstream, leptin makes the body feel full.

So experts have also reported that water fasting can make the body more sensitive to leptin and insulin: this means that the body is more efficient in reducing its blood sugar and hunger processing signals, and in turn, reduce obesity risk.

MAY REDUCE THE RISK OF MANY CHRONIC DISEASES

Some evidence suggests that water fasting could lower the risk of diseases like diabetes, cancer, and heart disease seen as chronic diseases.

Many animal studies have also linked water fasting to protection from damage to the heart by free radicals. **Free radicals-** being those *"unstable molecules that can damage parts of cells"* that contribute to these diseases. [20]

It could also suppress genes that help cancer cells grow; even improve the effects of chemotherapy.

Though most of these studies are based on animals, an adequate human study on water fasting is required before making recommendations. **Dangers or risks of water fasting**

Despite the numerous benefits, water fasting also has health risks, as outlined below:

LOSING THE WRONG TYPE OF WEIGHT

Because calories are restricted, you will lose weight fast while doing water fasting.

You may let go as much as 2 pounds (0.9 kg) of weight daily, from a 24hrs up to 72-hour water fast, the study suggests; unfortunately, this weight loss is mainly from water, carbs, and sometimes muscle mass.

DEHYDRATION

The research did suggest that about 20–30% of our daily water need comes from the foods we consume; so drinking only water and not eating meals can reduce the quantity of water needed by your body, thereby leading to dehydration.

You may be dehydrated if you're dizzy, having nausea, headaches, constipation, low blood pressure, reduced productivity, etc.

Orthostatic hypotension is known as *"a drop in blood pressure that happens when you suddenly stand up"*; it may lead to dizziness and even fainting.[21] If you notice this during a fast, ensure you avoid driving, operating heavyweight machinery to avoid an accident.

Medical conditions

It may also worsen many medical conditions. This is why people with medical conditions are advised the always seek advice before they start any fasting program.

Water fasting can inflate the level of uric acid production: a risk factor for **gout** attacks; high the risk of adverse side effects of type 1/ type 2 **diabetes.** It may also lead to eating disorders.

Finally, water fasting will help you lose weight, like every other kind of fasting, but this comes with its own risk, as stated above.

If you're considering benefiting from fasting as a weight-loss activity, you might want to do intermittent fasting rather than water fasting.

What you need to know about fasting fluids

There seems to be a kind of consensus on what constitutes fluids for fasting for all kinds of fasting, even for optional pediatric general anesthesia.

Let us examine the notable types of fasting fluids for all, especially those fasting for weight loss: Keto-Friendly drinks that are not water.

Types of fasting fluids different from water

Some people on a low carb and high fat keto diet wonder what they can drink apart from water. Although water is the best drink because it has no calorie, low carb drinks are an option.

Drinks with 0–5 grams of net carbs are the best option.

Hot drinks

Many hot drinks are said to be keto-friendly. You only need to be mindful of what you mix with it; things like whipping cream, zero-calorie sweeteners, unsweetened plant-based creamers, and sugar-free flavoring syrups are all good options.

1. BLACK /GREEN TEA

Tea is a regular option with a minor number of carbs: usually lower than 1 gram in each typical teacup (240 mL). Tea is calorie-free with a lot of **polyphenol antioxidants**.

2. COFFEE

Coffee is relatively free of calories and carbs; hence, suitable for the keto diet, just like tea. Its major content, caffeine, is good for metabolism. Coffee also gives **chlorogenic acid** and **polyphenol antioxidants**, which are good for weight loss.

3. HERBAL TEAS

Herbal teas are brews gotten from dried fruit, flowers, leaves, or herbs, like yerba mate, hibiscus, chamomile, peppermint, and rooibos tea.

The majority of these are low carbs, while some may have more carbs, so you may examine it before you drink.

Soft drinks

Most Soft drinks have a high sugar content that may be harmful, but ketofriendly options exist too, like:

ALTERNATIVE DIET SODAS

Generally, diet sodas, e.g., "Diet Coke" and "Diet Pepsi, are technically considered keto. They're not always the best choice because of artificial sweeteners, e.g., **sucralose** and **aspartame,** that could damage the gut's healthy bacteria.

Alternative diet sodas are produced with naturally gotten no-calorie sweeteners such as **stevia** or **erythritol**- sugar alcohol obtained from corn has fewer adverse effects than artificial sweeteners. Zevia and Virgil's Zero Sugar contents readily come to mind.

SPARKLING WATER

This is water carbonated with conventional mineral spring or carbon dioxide gas. Many sparkling water choices are seasoned but unsweetened. Hence, it's a low carb option. Keto-friendly sparkling waters like Aura Bora, Perrier, and Hint comes to mind.

Juices

As a rule, it's always good to avoid juice on keto; however, a few safe options exist. These are **lemon** and **lime fruit juices** low in carbs but packed with savor; you can always augment it with plain water or hot tea and related drink to liven up the flavor.

Few vegetable juices have a reduced level of carbs, and maybe among the keto diet, but always remember that juicing take out most of the nourishing fiber from the veggies unless you're taking the pulp. Keto-friendly vegetables that you can juice are **cucumber, celery, leafy greens**-kale, and spinach, but always check a label before using it to be sure it's not loaded with sugar or similar carb sources that you're avoiding.

Any of these with at least 10 grams of carbs is not suitable for keto.

Other fluids that are low in carbs and are keto-friendly, based on their compositions, are, e.g., certain Flavored waters, Milk alternatives, some Energy drinks, and Sports drinks.

Alcoholic beverages- Some alcoholic beverages are also good for ketosis. These are Low carb beer, Hard liquor(VodKa), and Low carb hard seltzer.

Keto Diet

The ketogenic, or keto, diet is used when referring to a diet with enough fats, moderate in protein, but low in carbs.

Traditionally use in treating epilepsy- a brain ailment that results in seizures.

Because of its therapeutic properties in handling epilepsy, the keto diet is reportedly capable of preventing or reducing the risk of other brain ailments, for instance, migraines.

The keto diet and migraine

In case you don't know yet, the Keto diet nutritional content consists primarily of fats and very few carbs that are lower than 50 grams per day.

An average American adult takes 200 to 350 grams of carbs each day; carbs are available in different foods: bread, fruits, pasta, cereals, milk and related dairy products, even starchy veggies like corn, potatoes, etc.

The human body is naturally programmed to start a metabolic condition known as ketosis once blood ketone levels increase beyond normal. These ketones, experts say, can protective against migraines.

Migraine is a condition that comes with headaches that could result in severe throbbing pain, most times on one side of the head; the ache can occur alongside other symptoms like sensitivity to light/sound, nausea, etc.

It's not yet clear what happens typically. Still, it's possible that the ketones created while on a keto diet bring back brain moodiness and energy metabolism to work against brain inflammation in migraine patients.

In a 2015 observational research, migraine frequency significantly dropped in women who maintained a low-calorie keto diet within a month against a normal low-calorie diet.

Again, women who maintain the keto diet reduce more weight, indicating that the lower migraine occurrence might be related to weight loss instead of the keto diet per se.

To ascertain if weight loss is related to lower migraine attacks, researchers did a follow-up learning. It showed that partakers with migraines had an average of 3 lesser occurrences in a month while on the low-calorie keto diet as against the low-calorie non-keto diet, even as both showed similar weight loss pattern.

A related study reported a significant decrease in migraine occurrence, interval, and severity after one month on the keto diet.

The keto diet could treat migraines but will not stop the condition entirely, as suggested by the facts available.

Does New Evidence suggest Keto Diet Increase Type 2 Diabetes Risk?

A new study that examined mouse discovers a possible risk in doing a popular diet. It's common knowledge that the keto diet is good for your health; a recent examination raises questions about its competence in causing type 2 diabetes.

Being on a low-carb and high-fat diet plan that makes the body break down fat rather than carbohydrates refers to **ketosis.** According to *The Journal of Physiology[23],* the findings linked the early phase of this diet to a boost in type 2 diabetes risk.

In collaboration with the *University Children's Hospital Zurich, ETH Zurich* did an examination; the mice were placed on ketogenic diets, highfat diets for metabolisms, and sugar reactions.

They observe that keto diets did not give room for the body to use insulin adequately, making it harder to control blood sugar naturally. This, they said, leads to insulin resistance that can increase the risk for type 2 diabetes.

Additional research is required to determine the mechanism surrounding the long-term effect of the diet on obesity.

"Although ketogenic diets are known to be healthy, our findings indicate that there may be an increased risk of insulin resistance with this type of diet that may lead to type 2 diabetes."

Christian Wolfrum, Ph.D., *a professor at ETH Zurich, noted. Wolfrum is also a co-author of the research.*

Another co-author of this examination, **Gerald Grandl**, Ph.D., *a professor at the German Research Center for Environmental Health, added* that he had earlier examined insulin resistance and keto diet.[22]

Examinations on mice provided dissimilar outcomes: It mainly preserved insulin in muscle and lessened glucose lenience methodically or in the liver only.

Doctors had earlier documented that fasting for some days, or being on a strict carbohydrate restriction, may result in **"starvation diabetes"** in dogs, rodents, and humans: Grandl relates this early study, a decade ago to these findings.

"No one will get type 2 diabetes while on keto, simply because the carb intake is not high enough to develop any form of hyperglycemia," Grandl said.

This means that the liver becomes insulin resistant; this he believes is reversible when the individual return to a high-carb, low/medium-fat diet, noting that carbs to a diet rich in fats are the wrong combination.

Dr. **Stephen Phinney,** the *co-founder and chief medical officer at Virta-* a program that asserts that it could reverse type 2 diabetes through drawing on ketosis, in his view noted that no available human study indicates a wellformulated keto diet can cause type 2 diabetes.[23]

"To the contrary, based upon many biomarkers that predict the incidence of type 2 diabetes, nutritional ketosis benefits all of them," he stated.

He argued that lots of research suggest carbohydrate restriction to help diabetes. He further noted that those with type 2 diabetes finding it difficult to adhere to a ketogenic diet is because they did not sustain the diet plan. Adhering to a ketogenic nutrition plan may be difficult, possibly because of misinformation on what constitutes a proper-formulated ketogenic diet.

"There is simply no 'one-size-fits-all' solution, making individualization extremely important," Phinney declared.

Research on mice is good but should not be conclusively attributed to humans.

S   T   :T

C   7

Spicy Chocolate Keto Fat Bombs

This meal has an overall preparation time of 8mins with 24 servings.

- Coconut oil: $\frac{2}{3}$cup.
- Suave peanut butter: $\frac{2}{3}$cup.
- Darkish cocoa: $\frac{1}{2}$cup.
- 4(6 g) packs stevia- for taste
- Ground cinnamon: 1 tbsp.
- Kosher salt: $\frac{1}{4}$ tsp.
- Coconut flakes: $\frac{1}{2}$cup, grilled.
- Cayenne: $\frac{1}{4}$tsp, for taste.

DIRECTIONS

- Mix Coconut oil and peanut butter with cocoa powder in a dual container, set atop of simmering water vessel; bake, occasionally whipping, until refined and smooth.

Put stevia, cinnamon, and salt together; stir to mix.

- Separate the blend among a silicone miniature muffin base, or line a miniature muffin container with liners and separate the blend among liners.

- Crest with coconut and cayenne before relocating it into a freezer, until firm: approximately 30mins.

Grilled Lemon Salmon

This meal has an overall preparation time of 27mins with four times servings.

- Fresh dill: 2 tsp.
- Pepper: $\frac{1}{2}$ tsp.
- Salt: $\frac{1}{2}$ tsp.
- Garlic powder: $\frac{1}{2}$ tsp.
- Salmon fillets: 1 $\frac{1}{2}$ lbs.
- Filled brown sugar: $\frac{1}{4}$ cup.
- 1 mixed chicken bouillon cube.
- Water: 3 tbsp.
- Oil: 3 tbsp.
- Soy Sauce: 3 tbsp.
- Nicely sliced green onions: 4 tbsp.
- Thinly cut lemon: 1
- Sliced onions: 2, divided into rings.

DIRECTIONS

- Spray dill, salt, pepper, and garlic powder atop salmon.
- Put in a narrow glass pan.
- Blend sugar, oil, chicken bouillon, soy sauce, together with green onions.
- Put atop salmon.
- Shield and freeze for 1 hr., to be turned, once.
- Trench to remove marinade.
- Place on grill, with moderate heat; put lemon and onion atop.
- Shield and boil for 15mins; or until fish is ready.

Avocado Quesadillas

This meal has an overall preparation time of 31mins with two times servings.

INGREDIENTS

- Vine-ripe tomatoes: 2, sowed and sliced into 1/4 inch fragments
- Ripened avocado:1, peeled, pockmarked, and sliced into 1/4 inch fragments
- Sliced red onion: 1 tbsp.
- New lemon juice: 2 tsp.
- Tabasco sauce: ¼tsp.
- Salt, pepper
- Sour cream: ¼ cup.
- Sliced fresh coriander: 3 tbsp.
- Flour Tortillas: 24 inches.
- Vegetable oil: ½tsp.
- Frayed Monterey jack cheese: 1 ⅓ cups.

DIRECTIONS

- With a little bowl, blend the tomatoes, avocado, onion, lemon together with juice and Tabasco.

Spice using salt and pepper: to taste.
-

- With a separate little bowl, blend sour cream, coriander together with pepper and salt: to taste.
- Place tortillas on a cooking pan and argument the top with oil. Broil
- tortillas 2 to 4 inches: from hot, until pale golden.
- Spray tortillas uniformly with cheese, broil until cheese smelt.
- Spread avocado blend uniformly atop 2 tortillas; crest each with 1 leftover tortilla and cheese side down to produce 2 quesadillas.
- Relocate quesadillas to a dividing board: sliced into 4 chunks.
- Crest each chunk with a spoon of the sour cream blend; serve warm.

Veggie Packed Cheesy Chicken Salad (Reduced Fat)

This meal has an overall preparation time of 35mins with one to two servings.

INGREDIENTS

- Prepared boneless without-skin chicken breast: 1 cup, cubed Celery,
- nicely sliced: ¼cup.
- Carrot: ¼cup, suave into ribbons.
- Baby Spinach: ½cup, roughly sliced
- Fat-free mayonnaise: 2 ½tbsp.
- Nonfat Sour Cream: 2 tbsp.
- Dried Parsley: ⅛ tsp.
- Dijon mustard: 2 tsp.
- Lessened-fat sharp cheddar cheese: ¼cup, frayed.

DIRECTIONS

- Blend ingredients in a bowl until all well coated with the mayonnaise combination.
- Cold in the fridge: at least 30mins; you may do this the night before.
- Serve.

Cobb Salad with Brown Derby Dressing

This meal has an overall preparation time of 30mins with two times servings.

INGREDIENTS

- Iceberg Lettuce: $\frac{1}{2}$ head.
- Watercress: $\frac{1}{2}$ cluster.
- Chicory lettuce: 1 cluster.
- Romaine Lettuce: $\frac{1}{2}$ head.
- Skinned and seeded moderate Tomatoes: 2
- Smoldered turkey breast: $\frac{1}{2}$ lb.
- Crisp Bacon: 6 cuts.
- Seeded and peeled avocado, divided into half:1
- 3 eggs: hardened.
- Chives: 2 tbsp., sliced well.
- Blue Cheese: $\frac{1}{2}$ cup, smashed.
  - DRESSING
- Water; 2 tbsp.
-
-
-
-
-
-
-
-
-

Sugar: $\frac{1}{8}$ tsp.

kosher salt: $\frac{3}{4}$ tsp.

Worcestershire sauce: $\frac{1}{2}$ tsp.

Balsamic vinegar/red wine vinegar: 2 tbsp.

New Lemon Juice: 1 tbsp.

New ground black pepper: $\frac{1}{2}$ tsp.

Dijon mustard: ⅛ tsp.

Olive Oil: 2 tbsp.

Garlic: 2 cloves, sliced well.

DIRECTIONS

- Cut all the greens well-almost minced.

Organize in rows with a relaxed salad container.

- Chop the tomatoes in half; seed, and cut well.
- Cubed the turkey, avocado, eggs with the bacon, well.
- Organize all ingredients, even the blue cheese: in rackets through the lettuces.

Spray it the chives.
.

. Bring to a table this way, before tossing with the dressing at last; serve in an ice-cold salad container. Serve with french bread: a fresh one.
.

. And for the DRESSING: join all ingredients minus the olive oil in a mixer and mix.

.

With the machine still running, gently put the oil and mix well. . Keep it cooled.

Note also that this dish is to be refrigerated; served as cooled as possible.

Vegan Fried 'Fish' Tacos

This meal has an overall preparation time of 50mins; yield: 8 little tacos.

INGREDIENTS

- Silken Tofu: 14 ounces.
- Panko Breadcrumbs: 2 cups.
- Plain Flour: ½ cup
- Salt: ½ tsp
- Smoldered paprika: 1tsp.
- Cayenne Pepper: ½ tsp,
- Ground Cumin: 1 tsp.
- Milk: ½ cup- non-dairy.
- Vegetable oil
- Cabbage: ¼ head, nicely frayed.
- Avocado:1, ripened.
- Little Tortillas: 8
- Vegan Mayonnaise: serving pickled onion
- Peeled Red Onion: 1, nicely sliced
- Apple Cider Vinegar: ¼ cup.
- Sugar: 1 tbsp.
- Salt: 1 tsp.

DIRECTIONS

- Tap the tofu with a few fragments of pantry spool to take out excess moisture; with a knife, cut the tofu into rough 1-inch lumps: make them flawed, not cubes, so that it may appear nice.

Put crumbs of bread into one wide, narrow bowl.
-
- Put flour, salt, smoldered paprika, cayenne, and cumin in a separate wide, narrow bowl and mix.

- Put the milk in a third wide, narrow bowl.
  Pick the lumps of tofu and lightly coat in the flour; add the milk and the crumbs of bread onto a baking pan.

- Pour vegetable oil: 1/2 -inch depth, into a deep frying saucepan; Put atop a medium heat, allow the oil to be hot, before spraying breadcrumb in it. When it starts bubbling and browning: the oil is very hot; add lumps of breaded tofu to the oil. Stir fry till golden underneath. Flip and boil, so it's evenly golden; take out to a baking pan lined with pantry spool to drain. Repeat the process for the remaining tofu.

On the Pickled Onion:

- Boil the apple cider vinegar added salt and sugar in a little vessel until sweltering. Put the nicely chopped red onion in a bowl and pour the warm vinegar atop. Allow to settle for at least 30mins; it softens and becomes pinkish.

- Serve hot fried tofu in warmed tortillas (using the appropriate stove) with pickled onion, a smudge of vegan mayo, frayed cabbage, and avocado.

Mediterranean Chicken Breasts with Avocado Tapenade

This meal has an overall preparation time of 15mins with four times servings.

INGREDIENTS

- Splits boneless Skinless Chicken Breast: 4 Chafed
- lemon peel: 1tbsp.
- Shared fresh lemon juice: 5 tbsp.
- Shared Olive Oil: 2 tbsp.
- Shared Olive Oil: 1 tsp.
- Garlic: 1 clove, nicely sliced.
- Salt: ½ tsp.
- Ground Black Pepper: ¼ tsp.
- heated and crushed Garlic: 2 Cloves.
- Sea Salt: ½ tsp.
- New Ground Pepper: ¼ tsp.
- Moderate tomatoes: 1, seeded and nicely chopped. ¼
- cup small green pimento-stuffed olive, thinly sliced
- Capers: 3 tbsp., washed.
- New basil leaves: 2 tbsp, nicely cut.
- 1 huge Hass avocado: ripened and nicely chopped

DIRECTIONS

- With a sealable malleable bag, mix chicken and marinade of lemon peel with 2 tbsp. of lemon juice and 2 tbsp. of olive oil; add garlic, salt, and pepper before sealing the bag for refrigeration for 30mins. . With a bowl, whip together leftover 3 tbsp. of lemon juice, baked garlic, and leftover 1/2 tsp. of olive oil; also put sea salt and fresh ground pepper. Blend with tomato, capers, basil, green olives, and avocado. Keep it aside.

Take out chicken from the bag, dispose of the marinade. Grill atop medium-hot coal: 4 to 5mins each side (to the desired degree of doneness).

- Serve with Avocado Tapenade.

MaMa's Supper Club Tilapia Parmesan

This meal has an overall preparation time of 35mins with four times servings.

INGREDIENTS

- Tilapia fillets: 2 lbs., or use orange roughy, cod, or red snapper.
- Lemon juice: 2 tbsp.
- Chafed parmesan cheese: ½ cup.
- Butter- room temperature: 4 tbsp.
- Mayonnaise: 3 tbsp.
- Nicely sliced green onions: 3 tbsp.
- Spicing salt: ¼ tsp. e.g., Old Bay seasoning.
- Dried basil: ¼ tsp.
- Black pepper
- Sprint hot pepper sauce:1

DIRECTIONS

- Preheat heater up to 350 degrees.
- With a buttered 13-by-9-inch sweltering plate (or jellyroll pan), place fillets in a solitary layer.
- Fillets are not to be stacked.
- Skirmish top with juice.
- With a bowl, blend cheese, butter, mayonnaise, onions, and spiced together.

With a fork, blend well.

- Overheat fish with preheated heater: 10 to 20mins (or until fish begins to flake).
- Spray with cheese blend; cook until golden brown: approximately 5mins.

Base sweltering time on the chunkiness of the fish used.

-
  - Examine fish well, so it doesn't overcook.
    Creates four servings.

Note: You can make the fish in a broiler too.

Broil: 3 to 4mins (or until almost ready).
-
  - Put cheese and broil extra 2 to 3mins (or until it's browned).

Shredded Brussels Sprouts With Bacon and Onions

This meal has an overall preparation time of 30mins with six times servings.

INGREDIENTS

- Bacon: 2 chunks.
- 1 sparingly cut little yellow onion.
- Salt: $\frac{1}{4}$tsp, for taste.
- Water: $\frac{3}{4}$cup.
- Dijon mustard: 1 tsp.
- Brussels sprout: 1 lb., thinly trimmed, halved, and well sliced
- Cider Vinegar: 1 tbsp.

DIRECTIONS

- Boil bacon with a huge skillet atop medium heat until crisp: 5 to 7mins; drain with paper towels before crumbling.
- Put onion and salt into drippings in the saucepan and boil atop medium heat, rousing regularly, until soft and browned: approximately 3mins.
- Put water and mustard, rasp up any browned morsel before adding Brussels sprouts; cook, rousing regularly, until soft: 4 to 6mins.
- Mix in vinegar and crest with already crumbled bacon.

Roasted Broccoli W Lemon Garlic & Toasted Pine Nuts

This meal has an overall preparation time of 22mins with four times servings.

INGREDIENTS

- Broccoli floret: 1lb.
- Olive Oil: 2 tbsp.
- Newly ground black pepper with salt.
- Unsalted butter: 2 tbsp.
- Garlic, minced: 1 tsp.
- Lemon zest-chafed: ½ tsp.
- Fresh Lemon Juice: between 1 -2 tbsp.
- Pine nuts, toasted: 2 tbsp.

DIRECTIONS

- Preheat heater up to 500 degrees.
- With a huge bowl, mix broccoli with the oil, salt, and pepper: for taste.
- Organize the florets in a solitary layer on a sweltering pan; roast, turning once: for 12mins or until soft.
- In the meantime, with a little saucepan, dissolve the butter atop medium heat.
- Put the garlic and lemon zest and boil, rousing for approximately a minute.

Allow cooling to some extent before mixing with the lemon juice. Put the broccoli in a serving container; dispense the lemon butter atop and toss to coat.

- Scatter crisped pine nuts atop the crest.

Cauliflower Popcorn - Roasted Cauliflower

This meal has an overall preparation time of 1hr 10mins with four times servings.

INGREDIENTS

- Cauliflower: 1 head, or pre-cut commercially prepped cauliflower of equivalent amount.
- Olive oil: 4 tbsp.
- Salt: 1 tsp., for taste

DIRECTIONS

- Preheat heater up to 425 degrees.
- Trim cauliflower head to remove the essential and dense stems. Slice florets into fragments like the size of "ping-pong" balls.
- With a huge bowl, mix the olive oil and salt; whip before adding the cauliflower pieces, then toss thoroughly.
- Line a sweltering pan with parchment for easy onslaught (you may ignore that if you don't have it); spread the cauliflower pieces on the pan and bake for 1 hour: rotating 3 or 4 times, until most of the pieces turned golden brown.

Note; The browner the pieces, the more caramelization occurs and the sweeter the taste.

- Serve instantly and enjoy.

Best Baked Potato

This meal has an overall preparation time of 1hr 10mins with a single serving.

INGREDIENTS

- Huge Russet Potato:1
- Canola Oil
- kosher salt

DIRECTIONS

- Scorch, the heater up to 350°F, place the racks atop and bottom thirds.
- Clean potato/potatoes well with a hard brush and icy running water.
- Dehydrate, before using a standard fork to poke 8 to 12 open holes on the spud. This allows moisture to escape while cooking.
- Put into a container and coat gently with oil.

- Spray with kosher salt. Put the potato on the rack and in the middle of the heater.
- Put a sweltering sheet (aluminum foil is ok) at the bottom of the rack to retain any drippings.
- Swelter for 1 hour or until the skin turns crunchy, with underneath flesh softened.
- Serve with a dotted line: an end to end with a fork; then crash the spud open by pressing each end with another.
- You will see pop right open.

- Though watch out for some steam.

NOTE: If you're using over 4 potatoes, you'll require an extended cooking time by up to 15mins.

Easy Black Bean Soup

This meal has an overall preparation time of 25mins with four times servings.

INGREDIENTS

- Olive Oil: 3 tbsp.
- Medium onion: 1 sliced.
- Ground cumin: 1 tbsp.
- Garlic: 2 to 3 cloves.
- Black Beans:2 (14 1/2 ounce) cans.
- 2 cups Chicken broth/Vegetable Broth
- Salt, pepper
- 1 little red Onion, well sliced.
- Cilantro: ¼ cup, nicely sliced.

DIRECTIONS

- Fry onion with olive oil.
- As the onion becomes glowing, put cumin.
- Bake for 30secs. Put garlic, and allow to heat for another 3060secs.
- Put 1contaniner of black beans and vegetable broth-2 cups.
- Get it to a simmer, rousing irregularly.
- Off the oven.
- With a hand mixer, mix ingredients in the pan, or relocate to a mixer.
- Put the second container of beans in the pan together with mixed ingredients and get it to simmer.
- Serve soup in a bowl of red Onion with Cilantro to garnish.

Vegan Lentil Burgers

This meal has an overall preparation time of 1hr 10mins and yields 8 to 10 burgers.

- Dry Lentils, adequately rinsed: 1cup.
- Water: 2 ½cups.
- Salt: ½ tsp.
- Olive Oil:1 tbsp.
- medium onion staked: ½
- Staked Carrot:1
- Pepper: 1 tsp.
- Soy Sauce: 1 tbsp.
- Rolled Oats: ¾ cup, nicely ground.
- Breadcrumbs: ¾ cup.

DIRECTIONS

- Cook lentils plus salt in the water: for about 45mins; lentils become soft and mostly free of water.
- Sauté the onions and carrot with oil until softened; for about 5mins.
- With a bowl, blend the baking ingredients with the pepper and soy sauce; also include oats, breadcrumbs.
- As still hot, make the blend into patties: this should give 8-10 burgers.
- Burgers will be shallow fried for 1 to 2mins on each side or bake at 200C for 15mins.

Vegan Coconut Kefir Banana Muffins

This meal has an overall preparation time of 45mins with 12 servings.

INGREDIENTS

- All-Purpose Flour: 2 cups.
- Granulated Sugar: 1 cup.
- Dried, frayed, unsweetened coconut: 1 cup.
- Baking Soda: 2 tsp.
- Baking Powder: 1 tsp.
- Salt: $\frac{1}{2}$ tsp.
- 2 ripened Bananas: crushed.
- Coconut milk: pc dairy-free kefir probiotic fermented, 1 $\frac{1}{2}$ cups.
- Cold-pressed watery coconut oil: $\frac{1}{4}$ cup.
- Vanilla Extract: 1 tsp.

DIRECTIONS

- Preheat the heater up to 350°F (180°C); Steam 12-count muffin tin in baking spray and keep aside.
- Whip together flour, coconut, sugar, baking soda, and baking powder; add salt in a huge bowl and keep it aside.
- Whip together the bananas, the kefir, and coconut oil with vanilla in a separate huge bowl; put flour blend and mix until white streaks disappear.
- Separate the prepared muffin tin; Bake until crests turn golden. Put a toothpick in its middle; allow about 30mins. Let it cool in a muffin tin: 15mins.

Cook's tip: in freezing muffins, allow them to cool completely on a rack before transferring to a secure container (re-sealable freezer bag), then freeze for up to a month: For better protection against freezer scorch, you may fold the muffins individually with plastic foil before you put in the can or bag. Melt muffins in the fridge immediate or microwave direct from ice-covered: until well warmed; for 20-30secs.

Egg Scramble with Sweet Potatoes

This meal has an overall preparation time of 25 mins, and a single serving.

INGREDIENTS:

- Staked sweet potato,1 (8-oz)
- Sliced onion, ½ cup
- Sliced rosemary, 2 tsp
- Salt
- Pepper
- Huge eggs, 4
- Huge egg whites, 4
- Sliced chive, 2 tbsp

DIRECTIONS:

1. Preheat the heater up to 425°F; on a baking pan, throw the sweet potato and onion with rosemary together; add salt, pepper. Spew with cooking spew, bake until soft: 20 minutes or so.
2. In the meantime, in a standard bowl: whip together egg whites, the eggs, and a taste of salt and pepper. Spritz a skillet with cooking spew, mix up the eggs on average for about 5 minutes.
3. Spray with sliced chives, serve with the spuds.

Each serving gives 571 calories, protein 44 g, carbs52 g: 9 g of fiber, with 20 g of fat.

Greek Chickpea Waffles

This meal has an overall preparation time of 30 mins, and two times servings.

INGREDIENTS:

- Chickpea flour: ¾ cup
- Baking soda: ½ tsp
- Salt: ½ tsp
- Pure 2% Greek yogurt: ¾ cup
- Huge eggs: 6
-

Use Cucumbers, Scallion, Tomatoes, Olive oil, and Parsley, plus Yogurt and Lemon juice when serving; though is optional

- Pepper and Salt

DIRECTIONS:

1. Preheat the heater up to 200°F; place a wireframe above a rimmed baking pan before placing it on the heater. Ignite a waffles iron for each direction.

2. With a huge bowl: whip together baking soda, flour, and salt. With a little basin, whip together eggs and the yogurt. Now blend the soaked ingredients into the dry element.

3. Calmly fleece the waffles iron with nonstick cooking spew. Batch by batch, fall ¼ to ½ cup hit into every segment of the iron; boil until it turns golden brown: 4 to 5mins. Relocate the waffles to the heater, let them remained warm. Do the same with a remaining hit.

4. Serve waffles with the salty tomato blend or sprinkle with temperate seed butter and berries.

Each serving gives 412 calories, 35 g protein, 24 g carbs: 4 g of fiber, with 18 g of fat.

PB&J Overnight Oats

This meal has an overall preparation time of 5 mins with 8 hours of refrigeration and single servings.

INGREDIENTS:

- Quick- cookery rolled oats: ¼ cup
- 2% milk: ½ cup
- Beige peanut butter: 3 tbsp
- Crushed raspberries: ¼ cup
- full raspberries: 3 tbsp

DIRECTIONS:

1. With a standard bowl, join the oats, peanut butter, milk, together with crushed raspberries: blend until smooth.
2. Wrap and refrigerate all night, uncover and top with full raspberries In the morning.

Each serving gives 455 *calories, protein* 20 g, *carbs* 36 g: 9 g *of fiber, with* 28 g *of fat.*

Turmeric Tofu Scramble

This meal has an overall preparation time of 15 mins, and a single serving.

INGREDIENTS:

- Portobello mushroom, 1
- Cherry tomatoes, 4 or 3
- Olive oil, 1 tbsp added extra for polishing
- Pepper and Salt
- Strong tofu, ½ block:14-oz
- Minced turmeric, ¼ tsp
- Touch garlic dust
- Lightly cut ½ avocado

DIRECTIONS:

1. Preheat the heater up to 400°F: on a baking pan, put the mushroom, tomatoes, and polish it with oil. Spice with pepper and salt. Bake until soft-10 minutes.

2. In the meantime, with a standard bowl: join the tofu, turmeric, and garlic dust with a pinch of salt. Puree with a fork; with a huge skillet above medium, warn a Tbsp of Olive oil; introduce the tofu mixture and boil; moving intermittently, until strong and egg-like: 3 mins or so.

3. Dish the tofu, served with mushroom and tomatoes, plus avocado.

Each serving gives 431 *calories,* 21 *g protein, carbs* 17 *g:* 8 *g of fiber, with* 33 *g of fat.*

Avocado Ricotta Power Toast

This meal has an overall preparation time of 5 mins, and a single serving.

INGREDIENTS:

- Whole-grain bread: 1 slice
- Splintered ripe avocado: ¼
- Ricotta: 2 tbsp
- Red pepper chips, squeeze crumpled
- Pinch chipped sea-salt

DIRECTIONS:

1. The Toasted bread is added with avocado, ricotta, and crumpled red pepper chips, including the sea salt. Consume with matted/hardened eggs to be served with yogurt/fruit.

2. *Each serving gives* 288 *calories, protein 10 g, carbs 29 g:* 10 *g of fiber, with* 17 *g of fat*

Turkish Egg Breakfast

This meal has an overall preparation time of 13mins with two times servings.

INGREDIENTS:

- Olive oil: 2 tbsp
- Cut up red bell pepper: ¾ cup
- Cut up eggplant: ¾ cup
- Pepper and salt: each, a Pinch
- 5 huge, lightly compressed eggs,
- Paprika: ¼ tsp
- Sliced cilantro to flavor
- Pure yogurt: 2 dollops
- A complete wheat pita:1

DIRECTIONS:

1. With a huge nonstick skillet on a moderately high, boil olive oil; add bell pepper, eggplant, and salt, also the pepper. Stir-fry until very soft: 7 minutes or so.
2. Blending with the eggs and paprika, also adding salt and pepper to flavor; boil, stirring regularly, until the eggs become softened and matted.
3. Smidgeon with sliced cilantro, serve with the pita, and a dollop of yogurt.

Each serving gives 469 calories, protein 25 g, carbs 26 g: 4 g fiber, and 29 g of fat.

Almond Apple Spice Muffins

This meal has an overall preparation time of 15mins with five times servings.

INGREDIENTS:

- Stick butter: ½
- Almond mealtime: 2 cups
- Vanilla protein powder: 4 measures
- Huge eggs: 4
- Un-sugared applesauce: 1 cup
- Cinnamon: 1 tbsp
- Allspice: 1 tsp
- Cloves: 1 tsp
- Baking powder: 2 tsp

DIRECTIONS:

1. Preheat the heater up to 350°F; with a little microwave-safe basin, soften the butter in the microwave: at a low temperature for about 30 seconds.
2. With a huge bowl, mix all remaining ingredients thoroughly together with the softened butter. Sprig 2 muffin tins with nonstick cookery spray/use cupcake liners.
3. Transfer the mixture into the muffin tins and ensure not to overfill: about ¾ full; 10 muffins is fine.
4. Put one tray in the heater and overheat for 12 minutes. Ensure not to over-heat, as the muffins will turn too dehydrated. When baked, remove the initial tray from the heater and roast the second muffin tin similarly, too.

Each serving gives 484 calories, protein 40 g, carbs 16 g: 5 g fiber, and 31 g of fat.

C 9D   R

Turkey Tacos

This meal has an overall preparation time of 25 minutes and four times servings.

INGREDIENTS:

- Oil: 2 tsp
- Sliced little red onion,
- 1 excellently sliced section of garlic
- More-lean crushed turkey:1 lb.
- Taco seasoning: sodium-free, 1 tbsp
- Hot whole-grain corn tortillas: 8
- Sour cream: ¼ cup
- Ragged Mexican cheese: ½ cup
- Chopped avocado:1
- Sliced lettuce: 1 cup
- and Salsa: for serving

DIRECTIONS:

1. With a huge skillet on moderately high, boil the oil. Put onion and heat, moving until very soft: 5 to 6mins. Blend with the garlic and boil for 1minute.

2. Put the turkey and boil, use a spoon to scatter it, and watch it turn almost brown: 5 minutes. Put the taco seasoning and water- 1 cup. Smolder until reduced to a little more than half- 7 minutes.

3. Load the tortillas with turkey, crest with cheese, avocado, sour cream, lettuce, and salsa.

Each serving gives 472 calories, protein 28 g, carbs30 g: 6 g fiber, and 27 g of fat.

Healthy Spaghetti Bolognese

This meal has an overall preparation time of 1 hr. 30mins with four times servings.

INGREDIENTS:

- Huge spaghetti squash: 1
- Olive oil: 3 tbsp
- Garlic powder: ½ tsp
- Kosher salt, pepper
- 1 little onion: well sliced
- Crushed turkey: 1¼ lb.
- finely sliced garlic cloves: 4
- Little cremini mushrooms: 8 oz., chopped.
- New staked tomatoes: 3 cups- or 2 (15-oz) cans.
- 1 (8-oz) can little-sodium, sugar-free plus tomato sauce.
- New sliced basil.

DIRECTIONS:

1. Preheat the heater up to 400°F; slice the spaghetti squash by half laterally and remove seeds. Brush each half with 1/2 tbsp oil, garlic powder, and spice with ¼ tbsp of salt and pepper. Put skin-side upward onto a rimmed baking pan; bake until soft- 35 to 40mins. Allow to unruffled for 10mins.

2. In the meantime, with a huge skillet on moderate, boil the 2 Tbsp of oil, adding onion, season, and ¼ tsp each of salt, pepper, before cooking, occasionally turning, until soft: 6mins. Add turkey and boil; scatter into little pieces with a spoon until browned: 6 to 7mins. Blend with the garlic and boil for: 1 minute.

3. Shove the turkey combination to one side of the saucepan, and then mix the mushrooms with the other. Boil, occasionally move, until the mushrooms become soft: 5mins. Join with the turkey. Put the tomatoes and tomato sauce, now simmer up to 10mins.

4. As the sauce simmers, measure out the squash and relocate to plates. Dollop the turkey Bolognese atop and spray with basil, as desired.

Each serving gives 450 calories, protein 32 g, carbs31 g: 6 g fiber, and 23 g of fat.

Chicken with Fried Cauliflower Rice

This meal has an overall preparation time of 35mins with four times servings.

- Grape seed oil: 2 tbsp
- Chicken breast without bone and skin: 1 ¼ lb., pounded to the equal chunkiness
- 4 huge eggs: flattened
- Nicely sliced red bell peppers: 2
- 2 little carrots: nicely sliced
- Nicely sliced onion: 1
- Garlic: 2 cloves, nicely sliced.
- Nicely sliced scallions: 4, add extra for serving.
- Frozen peas: ½ cup, melted
- Cauliflower "rice": 4 cups.
- Soy sauce-low in sodium: 2 tbsp
- Rice vinegar: 2 tsp
- Kosher salt, pepper

DIRECTIONS:

1. With a huge, deep skillet atop a moderate-high, make-hot 1 tbsp oil. Put chicken, boil until golden brown: 3 to 4mins each side. Relocate to a dividing board and allow to settle for 6mins, then slice. Put the remaining 1 tbsp oil into the skillet; with the eggs, scramble until it setS, 1 to 2mins before relocating to a bowl.

2. Put bell pepper, carrot, and onion in the skillet and boil, often turning until soft: 4 to 5mins. Blend with garlic and boil: 1 minute and toss together with scallions and peas.

3. Put together cauliflower, soy sauce, and rice vinegar with salt and pepper before tossing to mix. Allow the cauliflower to settle, without rousing, and watch it turn brown: 2 to 3mins; toss with the minced eggs and chicken.

Each serving gives 427 calories, protein 45 g, carbs 25 g: 7 g fiber, and 16 g of fat.

Sheet Pan Steak

This meal has an overall preparation time of 50Mins with four times servings.

- Little cremini mushrooms: 1 lb., trimmed and shared.
- Trimmed Bunch broccolini: 1 ¼ lb., divided into 2-inches
- size. Garlic: 4 cloves, nicely sliced Olive oil: 3 tbsp.
- Skick.
- Kosher salt, pepper
- 1-inch in thickness-New York strip steaks: 2 approximately 1½ lb
- in all, with excess fat trimmed.
- 1 15-oz can little-sodium cannellini beans: washed.

DIRECTIONS:

1. Preheat the heater up to 450°F; with a luge rimmed baking pan, toss the mushrooms with broccolini, garlic, oil, and red pepper flakes, including ¼ tsp of salt and pepper. Put the baking pan in the heater and bake 15mins.

2. Shove the mixture at the edges of the saucepan so you can work on the steaks. Spice the steaks using ¼ tsp of salt, pepper before placing in the saucepan center; Bake the steaks to required doneness: 5 to 7mins each side for moderate-rare. Then relocate the steaks to a dividing board and allow to settle: 5mins and slice.

3. Put beans in the baking pan and toss to mix: Bake until well heated: approximately 3mins; Serving with vegetables, beans, and steaks.

Each serving gives 464 calories, protein 42 g, carbs 26 g: 8 g fiber, and 22 g of fat.

Pork Tenderloin with Butternut Squash and Brussels Sprouts

This meal has an overall preparation time of 50mins with| four times servings

INGREDIENTS:

- Shaved pork tenderloin: 1 ¾ lb.
- Salt, Pepper
- Canola oil: 3 tbsp.
- New thyme: 2 stems
- Skinned Garlic: 2 cloves
- Brussels sprouts: 4 cups, shaved and shared
- Butternut squash: 4 cups, staked.

DIRECTIONS:

1. Preheat the heater up to 400°F; Spice the tenderloin with salt, pepper. With a huge cast-iron pan atop the moderate-high heat, boil 1 tbsp. of oil, and then add the tenderloin when the oil shimmers. Burn until golden brown on each side: 8 to 12mins. Relocate to a dish.

2. Put the thyme, garlic, and remaining 2 tbsp oil into the pan; boil until scented, approximately 1 minute. Put the Brussels sprouts and the butternut squash with a large pinch of salt, pepper. Boil, occasionally rousing until the vegetables turn a little brown: 4 to 6mins.

3. Put the tenderloin above the vegetables, relocate all into the heater, and boil until vegetables become soft; insert a meat thermometer into the thickest section of the tenderloin and take note of 140°F: 15 to 20mins.

4. Wearing heater paws, gently take down the pan from the heater; let the tenderloin settle: for 5mins, then slice; and serve with the vegetables. Toss greens with balsamic vinaigrette to serve. Each serving gives 401 calories, protein 44 g, carbs 25 g: 6 g fiber, and 15 g of fat.

Wild Cajun Spiced Salmon

This meal has an overall preparation time of 30mins with four times servings.

INGREDIENTS:

- Wild Alaskan Salmon fillet: 1½ lb.
- Spice: sodium-free taco
- Cauliflower: ½ head- about 1 lb., chopped into buds
- Broccoli: 1 head- about 1 lb., chopped into buds
- Olive oil: 3 tbsp.
- Garlic powder: ½ tsp.
- Diced tomatoes: 4 middle size

DIRECTIONS:

1. Preheat the heater up to 375°F; Put the salmon on a cooking plate. With a little bowl, blend the taco spice with ½ cup of water; put the mixture atop the salmon, cook until opaque everywhere: 12 to 15mins.

2. In the meantime, with a food processor- in batches, as needed, beat the cauliflower, broccoli until nicely sliced and "riced."

3. With a huge skillet on moderate, burn the oil, adding the cauliflower, broccoli, and sprinkle with garlic powder before cooking. Toss until it becomes soft: 5 to 6mins.

4. Serve salmon on top of "rice" and top with tomatoes.

Each serving gives 408 calories, protein 42 g, carbs 9 g: 3 g fiber, and 23 g of fat.

Pork Chops with Bloody Mary Tomato Salad

This meal has an overall preparation time of 25mins with four times servings.

INGREDIENTS:

- Olive oil: 2 tbsp.
- Red wine vinegar: 2 tbsp.
- Worcestershire sauce: 2 tsp.
- Ready horseradish: 2 tsp., pressed dry.
- Tabasco: ½ tsp.
- Celery seeds: ½ tsp.
- Kosher salt.
- Shared cherry tomatoes: 1 pint.
- Thinly chopped celery stalks: 2
- Little red onion: ½, thinly chopped
- Little bone-in pork chops: 4-1 inch in thickness, approximately 2¼ lb., all.
- Pepper
- Nicely sliced flat-leaf parsley: ¼ cup.
- Torn little head of green-leaf lettuce:1

DIRECTIONS:

1. Heat grill to moderate high; with a huge bowl, whip the oil, vinegar, Worcestershire sauce, and horseradish together with Tabasco and celery seeds. Add ¼ tsp of salt and toss with the tomatoes, onion, and celery.
2. Spice the pork chops with ½ tsp of salt and pepper; grill until golden brown, then cook for 5 to 7mins each of the sides.
3. Bend the parsley in the tomatoes, serve atop pork, greens, and consume with crushed cauliflower or potatoes.

Each serving gives 400 calories, protein39 g, carbs 8 g: 3 g fiber, and 23 g of fat.

CPSIA information can be obtained
at www.ICGtesting.com
Printed in the USA
LVHW061657120621
690060LV00008B/857